# Deprivation Trauma

*A Transpersonal Approach To Healing*

To Evelyn,

With Love
and Best Wishes

Zalora Fay Price

P.S. Loved our time together!

# Deprivation Trauma

*A Transpersonal Approach To Healing*

*A look at life at the soul level*

## Zalora Price

PUBLICATIONS

Victoria, Texas

Copyright © 2006 by Zalora Price

All rights reserved. No part of this book may be reproduced by any mechanical, photographic, or electronic process or in the form of a photographic recording; nor may it be stored in a retrieval system, transmitted, or otherwise be copied for private or public use - other than for "fair use" as brief quotations embodied in articles and reviews without prior written permission of the publisher.

The intent of the author is only to offer information of a general nature to help you in your quest for emotional and spiritual well-being. In the event you use any of the information in this book for yourself, which is your constitutional right, the author and the publisher assumes no responsibility for your actions.

Laurel Publications
6029 Country Club Drive
Victoria, Texas 77904

ISBN 0-9779932-0-5
ISBN 0-9780-9779932-0-8

Printed in the United States of America

# *Contents*

| | |
|---|---|
| Foreword | 13 |
| Introduction | 17 |

## Part I: Consciousness

*Knowing* — 25

    Chapter 1
        Aristotle, Cicero, Kant, and Emerson — 27
    Chapter 2
        Let's Keep it Simple — 33
    Chapter 3
        Simplified Stages of Consciousness — 37
        Simple Consciousness — 38
        Self Consciousness — 38
        Higher Consciousness — 42
    Chapter 4
        There is More — 46

## Part II: Deprivation
    "Stories of Fay"

*Sea glass* — 51

Prelude — 53

    Chapter 1
        The Spirit Has Landed — 57
    Chapter 2
        From the Minds of Babes — 62

Chapter 3
- Continuity of Life — 68

Chapter 4
- Joining the Family — 72

Chapter 5
- Opposites Attract — 76

Chapter 6
- Life Gets Worse — 79

Chapter 7
- From County to Town — 87

Chapter 8
- I Didn't Know I Could Not Fly — 91

Chapter 9
- Daddy Comes Home — 95

Chapter 10
- Move to Missouri — 102

Chapter 11
- Disaster — 106

Chapter 12
- Time Again For School — 110

Chapter 13
- I Could Hold My own — 118

Chapter 14
- A Step Forward, A Step Back — 122

Chapter 15
- Those Pesky Mosquitoes — 129

Chapter 16
- Petty's Place — 133

Chapter 17
- Lessons on Charity — 146

Chapter 18
- Turning Point — 150

Chapter 19
- The Good and the Bad — 161

Chapter 20
    Day Hands                      165
Chapter 21
    Reassured                      168
Chapter 22
    Welfare                        174
Chapter 23
    Remembering                    178
Chapter 24
    A New Life                     181
Chapter 25
    A Look Back                    185
Chapter 26
    Something Has Got To Give      189
Chapter 27
    Coming of Age                  198
Chapter 28
    Time to Move On                201
Chapter 29
    My First Job                   206
Chapter 30
    He Got His Revenge             213
Chapter 31
    Mother Returns                 217
Chapter 32
    Taken in from the Cold         221
Chapter 33
    Pulled into the Social Group   229
Chapter 34
    Religion                       235
Chapter 35
    My Senior Year                 239
Chapter 36
    Moving On                      245

Chapter 37
   The Universe Sings      248

Epilogue

# Part III: Transformation

Chapter 1
   My Soul, My Spirit, My Self      259
Chapter 2
   The Process of Healing      267
     Step 1
     - Life is a process.      268
     Step 2
     - Healing is an inside job.      270
     Step 3
     - Leave the disfunctioning part of
       yourself/life behind.      271
     Step 4
     - Unload, sort out, and get a grip
       on things.      272
     Step 5
     - We are controlled by our beliefs.      272
     Step 6
     - Take care of yourself, before you try
       to care for others.      273
     Step 7
     - Set reasonable goals.      274
     Step 8
     - Open yourself to life's experiences.      275
     Step 9
     - Develop awareness.      276

Step 10
- 'Coping Skills,' 'Survival Skills,' and 'Defense Mechanisms' are not dirty words.     278

Step 11
- Forgiveness.     279

*Pass Me By*     282

Step 12
- Make 'Transpersonal' a word in your vocabulary.     283

*Light Came A'Creeping*     285

Appendix 1 - Worksheet     287

Acknowledgements     289

About the Author     291

# Foreword

# Foreword

The year was 1977. It was a warm summer day. I had just stepped into a refreshing shower. I stood with my head tossed backward under the running water and reveled in the feeling of the warm water cascading over my head and shoulders, caressing my head and body.

As we all do, I closed my eyes to soak up the sensation....and found myself standing in a large, open field. I looked around me in surprise. Everything seemed brighter than usual. And I felt an unusual sense of wellness and calmness. I felt something in my hand and looked down with curiosity. I was holding a book.

My attention focused on the book. For some reason, I was holding the book with its back side up. I didn't stop to read the back cover. I just turned the book over while thinking, "Nice book, nice cover." Then, I stared at the front cover. Written across the top were the words, 'Deprivation Trauma.' Below in script was written, 'A Transpersonal Approach to Healing.' And, further down the cover, written in even smaller print, were the words, 'Autobiography of Fay Johnson' (my maiden name).

I was stunned. Why would anyone want to read a book about my life? As I stared at the book, a voice said, "If you write it, it will be published."

I blinked....and I was back in the shower.

I turned off the water and grabbed a towel.

I dried myself quickly and wrapped a robe around myself as I hurried to my study. I immediately sketched the front of the book. As I wrote in the title words, I realized that the book was not about me. It was about my "story." The 'story' of my life as it relates to the story of other lives. It was about my consciousness and my healing. It was about the transformation possible to all who increase their level of consciousness, and the healing that takes place as a natural conclusion to the process.

The vision of the book was gone. I had not read the back

cover for any other details of the book. But my mind immediately formulated a chart showing five areas of deprivation: physical, emotional, social, educational, and spiritual. And I knew that the resulting trauma did not come from the customary 'abuse' associated with trauma, but from the long term deprivation associated with each of these five areas in my life.

In each of these five areas I was deprived of a life that would be considered 'normal' within our society. This kind of trauma covered a much larger scope of life than a single event or episode. A scope not usually associated with trauma. The trauma of which I speak developed from prolonged series of events. These events caused me pain, and brought anger and fear into my life.

I had to fight with my family for my education while I suffered both physically and emotionally from their abuse, and this was followed by my being rejected socially by the outside world. My trauma developed because my personal power was taken away through isolation and an over-powering parent, my mother, and a sibling, my brother. I suffered social rejection when I was exposed to the outside world. Because of my years of isolation, I became 'out of touch' with reality, especially in the social and spiritual realms. This resulted in my not knowing social customs or who I could turn to for comfort and support.

My book is for everyone who feels alone in their struggle to understand life and with the assurance that you can regain your personal power and enrich your life and your health by learning to make conscious choices based upon your Soul's needs.

# Introduction

# Introduction

My hypothesis is that consciousness (awareness) is the forerunner of all true healing. If you have no understanding of what is taking place in your life (other than that life is simply happening) you have no way to know how to make corrections for growth. That is why I chose to begin my stories with Part One, Chapter 1 (Let's Keep it Simple) to give a very brief introduction to Consciousness. And while the subject matter is over-simplified, it does give a working knowledge for reference.

I begin this work with 'consciousness' to provide a tool. This tool, the awareness of our consciousness, can be used to facilitate healing. Specifically, when we are consciously aware of our emotional responses to situations, circumstances, and attitudes, and understand how our belief systems and the ideas we have about our lives affect us, we are on the path to making the right choices to healing and having a more joyful life. This applies whether this healing is of the mind or of the body.

I hope the simplicity of this part of the book will act as a primer to you and to encourage you to further explore the many volumes that are available on consciousness.

Part One, Chapter 2 (There Is More) asks us to stop a moment and consider our philosophy on life. Then consider if we are open to personal growth.

The verse, "Knowing," at the beginning of Part One, was composed by me in February, 1991, after one of my "Universal Experiences" that also included a vision. "Universal/Peak Experiences" are experienced by many. Yet when we try to explain what we have experienced, words in our English vocabulary do not seem sufficient to cover the event and content. I felt the need to share it along with the other verse that I have included. The other verses came about also through personal experiences. Verse is sometimes skipped over when you are simply trying to get the essence of a story. But in a sense it is also another level of 'who I am;' and I am sharing me with the reader.

Part Two of the book is reminiscent of a case study revolving around (me) Fay Johnson. Fay's stories address five areas of trauma in my younger life. They are: physical, emotional, educational, social, and spiritual; with each area contributing to the deprivation of a life that would be considered normal within our society. With starvation, physical abuse, lack of education, and limited possibilities, I struggled forward, waiting for the day to come when I could move on to a more rewarding life.

To detail how I constantly had to 'dodge the bullets' of hand slaps, fists, and other objects, suffer verbal abuse, endure loneliness, and live a life of faith and hope that were not validated by religion or spiritual knowledge are not within the scope of the book. The stories presented were chosen because they are appropriate in showing the five areas of long term deprivation. To tell OF them is enough. This is because the stories are not about Fay, per se, but about my awareness and eventual healing through the transcendent self. Throughout the stories, the five areas of deprivation and trauma I experienced are cumulative in nature and presented as they occurred in the chronological order of my life.

While my awareness at such an early age would be considered atypical to many, my thought processes are so simple that anyone can learn to live more consciously by following my example of mentally 'being present' each moment of our lives. I was aware that I had a choice in choosing how I would react to my circumstances. I could look at it emotionally or logically. It was common sense to me at the time to sort it out in my head rather than becoming emotionally upset. And I have since found out, health wise, how my physical health has surpassed those that have chosen to live with anger, fear, and unforgiveness. I also considered the world and the universe in relationship to my small existence. I tried to see the 'big' picture. This gave me insight and hope that things could change if I did my part.

I drew on my innate intelligence and self-awareness. I developed out of necessity, coping mechanisms, interpersonal skills and survival skills. These skills are not specific to me. They are common to survivors of traumatic lives. Each tool/skill was challenged daily in my life. I will talk more about the use of them in the twelve step process for transformation found in Part Three of this book.

I have provided a chart at the end of the book (Appendix 1) for you to list experiences and skills you identified while reading my story that you used in your life that may have brought you survival or helped you to be where you are today. By doing so, you are giving a simple acknowledgement of what has taken place in your life. This self-analysis can also be used as a work plan for personal growth.

Part Three, Chapter 1 "My Soul, My Spirit, My Self" reflects my own experiences and understanding of Soul, Spirit, Self. I have attempted to explain the belief system of how, as spiritual beings on this physical journey, and as a true non-dual Self (not separated from our Source), we can live lives that are wonderfully fulfilling while living in a very complex society.

I speak of "My Soul, My Spirit, My Self" as the Essence that dwells within, that eternal (Soul) Spirit and vibrant personality that reaches out and touches lives: All that embodies me! All that embodies you! It is that greater part of us that came to live in a carnal mass and to give it 'life.' I believe it has a purpose and our lives are never satisfied until we follow our hearts to find that purpose. To find our paths we must follow Spirit because our Spirit is our real Self.

Within the context of Part Three, Chapter 1 (My Soul, My Spirit, My Self) I introduce my concerns for the needs within our present society and how we can use our consciousness to transcend our environment and to create good health. I also give ideas and information to facilitate healing through raising our individual level of consciousness.

Part Three, Chapter 2 (The Process of Healing) is a look

at the way we can facilitate living more consciously to expedite transcendence, via a twelve step process. These steps can help bring you to the point where you can become your own counsel and can travel your "path" by conscious choices and inner strength. You can change who you think you are by looking at life at the soul level.

My sincere purpose is to bring to you ideas that will broaden your perception of this journey we travel together, adding to your life and to those you love.

Zalora Price

# PART I

# *Consciousness*

# Knowing

*I open myself, and the universe pours in.*
*Why me?*
*A "seeker?" Yes.*
*I did not understand that which I asked.*
*I cannot be the same.*
*And I have no words to help you grasp*
*the magnitude of my 'knowing.'*

~ Zalora Price, February 1991 ~

# Chapter 1

## Aristotle, Cicero, Kant, and Emerson

The book is first and foremost a memoir. No attempt has been made to be an authority on any one of the philosophical, psychological, or spiritual concepts addressed. The definitions used are for the simple understanding of where I am going and/or taking the reader on this journey.

I have resorted to 'name dropping' to show that my ideas are not new ones. While I wish they were my own ideas and concepts, I am in fact merely borrowing them to put some understanding to life and experiences.

When I began to look back on my life I had many questions. The questions I asked most often that started me on this journey of writing about my life were, "What is the source of our vocabulary (which resulted after a 'peak experience' and I had no words to explain it)? Does the working knowledge of a word imply its true and complete meaning in all societies? How did our thought processes (use of words) concerning the study of our mind and soul come to us?" In other words, our whole concept of our world and our lives are reflected by the intention of our vocabulary. And I reasoned that mankind needed to take "soul" out of the strictly religious framework and put it into a working understanding of everyday life. I want it to be recognized as our wonderful true self that does not need to carry the guilt and shame associated with sin (separation from God) advocated by the church. I want our souls to be recognized as ourselves to be nurtured for our fullest human potential.

Going back in history I found that Aristotle's interpreted works indicate that he spoke of consciousness and the soul. Socrates and Plato addressed the body, mind, and spirit. These ancient ancestors worshiped many Gods and may have looked at things a little different within the framework of their society. Ancient Hebrew and many other religious and philosophical traditions often consider the soul (spirit) as the true basis for sentience in a living being. This concept we recognize and accept in religion today.

The words soul, spirit, psyche (mind), consciousness, originated in the early Ancient Greek philosophy around 500 B.C. (recorded philosophical history is a little sketchy before then) and the word consciousness was later found in the writings of Cicero (Latin) around 100 B.C. The words were carried down through the centuries within the context of law, philosophy, religious thought and doctrines. During this time frame mankind was interested in developing a moral and orderly society. Cicero, himself, used the word consciousness in trying to ascertain if man knew he was breaking the law. Similarly, the ancient religions of the world still observed today (incl. Jainism, Hindi, Judaism, Buddhism, Baha'ism, Islam, and Christianity), all contain some concept of soul and/or spirit.

In this book I am taking these same words (concepts) and applying them within the context of an individual's life instead of that as a culture. Cultural things like morality, religious worship, and law may not be sufficient for understanding and satisfaction in some people's lives. When man feels that he needs more to understand life and his mortality, he will seek within.

The extent of our knowledge and understanding is found 'within' our consciousness. Soul and consciousness are used interchangeably throughout literature. To accept one's consciousness as the seat of the soul gives us a place to go for understanding and enlightenment. It may not be a priority today but when our consciousness and awareness of ourselves and our world expands, we may be able to transcend our limitations as human beings. Or, as some advocate, we may see an evolution of mankind.

The word transcendental, or transcendence, originated as a Latin word in ancient philosophy and implied the concept of climbing or going beyond. It came into prominence in America through the works of German philosopher Immanuel Kant (1724-1804).

Immanuel Kant used the word 'transcendental' in a written reply to the philosopher Locke (who believed that there was nothing in our intellect that had not been put there by experiences) stating that there was a very important class of ideas which did not come from experiences but through which experiences were acquired. He said that these were intuitions of the mind and called them transcendental forms of thought. He also emphasized the power of the mind in shaping our experiences.

Kant's work was well respected by American philosophers Emerson and Thoreau and influenced their ideology. Ralph Waldo Emerson wrote and presented a paper in 1842 called The Transcendentalist. In it he emphasized intuitive thought and called it transcendental. At the time, both he and Thoreau were taking exception with the church on many issues. At the forefront was the concept of self or the individual. Up until the 17th century the church and political systems had taken away much personal freedom from the populace. Both Emerson and Thoreau advocated the return of these personal and individual freedoms and further extolled the value of going back to nature.

Together with Sarah Margaret Fuller (1810-1850) they started the Transcendentalists Newspaper in Massachusetts. Margaret Fuller not only helped with the production of the paper but also wrote for the paper. A prevalent message in the paper centered on the divinity of each individual. This divinity could only be identified if the individual had the independence of mind to act accordingly. This individualism meant listening to man's inner voice and being guided by intuition. Further, they advocated, there is meaning in everything. All meaning and everything in life was good because it was part of a divine plan. That divine plan provides a divine spark within each of us and connects everything and everybody, including the environment.

Transcendentalism has been designated as a spiritual movement. But it sparked ideas on the development of the individual mind and personal liberty. A wide spread interest in self-development and human experiences occurred through the movement. Much of the philosophy from the sixteenth to the twentieth century had been trying to conceptualize how the mind knows the world, the divine, and itself. The writings from this period can fill libraries. And many theories were issued. While William James (1842-1910) spoke of 'selective consciousness and the will,' Freud (1856-1939) was coining the terms 'ego, superego, and id.' Jung (1875-1961) meanwhile was presenting the idea of 'collective unconscious,' Maslowe (1908-1970) spoke of 'peak experiences and self-actualization,' and Assagioli (1888-1974) started 'psychosynthesis' (synthesis - bringing together a scientific approach which encompassed the whole man). It was during this time that a vocabulary and a foundation were laid for the development of a field of psychology called Transpersonal Psychology. There were others involved then and now who have made significant contributions.

The word psyche from classical Greek is interpreted to mean 'soul' or 'mind'. The meaning of 'logos' is 'the study of'. Therefore, we have (Trans) going through or above the Personal (self) to study the mind/soul. Scientifically speaking, the field of psychology does not study the soul since there is as yet no "acceptable" empirical evidence to prove that the soul exists. Like electricity, radio waves, and the wind, we can only look at divinity and its effects on individuals and the world and know that we have something worthy of our attention.

To study the mind and soul, psychologists have turned to measuring consciousness. While some say that consciousness is merely a neural functioning of the brain that dictates the way we experience the world, others say that consciousness is the seat of the soul and that the soul is put there to lead and direct our lives. I believe that both definitions have merit. Each definition of consciousness serves a necessary function in our lives – physical functioning and spiritual wellness. This concept of the importance and dependency on the relationship between Consciousness and Soul to our lives is the foundation upon which this book is built.

# Chapter 2

## Let's Keep it Simple

Consciousness/awareness/unconsciousness/superconsciousness/collective unconscious/soul/self-actualization has been in our vocabulary as common use words since Carl Gustav Jung, and the writings of William James (considered the father of American psychology), Roberto Assagioli, Abraham Maslow, Stanislav Grof, Anthony Sutich, and many others at the time and that followed. They provided the concepts and vocabulary. In this sense they were the beginners for the movement that formulated the foundation for the first Transpersonal Psychologist. During a meeting of a small working group in 1967 looking at the new discipline that would honor the entire spectrum of human experience, including various non-ordinary states of consciousness, Stan Grof suggested the name "Transpersonal." A new discipline was born.

Transpersonal Psychology is an academic discipline. The Transpersonal Psychology Departments in universities today differentiate themselves from other fields of psychology by including aspects of spirituality in the study of psychology. But the Journal of Transpersonal Psychology, which was initiated in 1969 by Abraham Maslow, Stanislav Grof and Anthony Sutich, suggests a further definition. "Transpersonal Psychology is concerned with the study of humanity's highest potential, and with the recognition, understanding, and realization of unitive, spiritual, and transcendent states of consciousness" (Lajoie and

Shapiro, 1992:91).

Transpersonal psychology is sometimes confused with parapsychology (paranormal, supernatural) because of the research interest of both fields of study. It is sometimes confused with New Age. But New Age is a spiritual movement and not an academic discipline. It is not Epistemology. Epistemology is a branch of philosophy that deals with the nature, origin, and scope of knowledge. Transpersonal Psychology stands alone as a discipline but its research reaches across a wide spectrum of investigations.

Paving the way for the development of transpersonal psychology were the Philosophers and the Transcendentalists like Emerson and Thoreau who in the early 1900's brought us the philosophy that what comes first in life is the spiritual which is followed by the transcendence over the material and empirical. In this philosophy, to transcend was to rise above or go beyond the limits of ordinary experiences. To put this concept into a more personal sense, we can experience the 'transpersonal' by going consciously beyond the physical self.

Edgar D. Mitchell was an Apollo 14 Astronaut to the Moon in February, 1971. On his return flight back to Earth he reported having what I would call a 'peak' experience. You might also call it an 'altered state of consciousness.' He felt a sense of interconnectedness of things in the Universe. And it changed his life forever. Subsequently, he formed the Institute of Noetic Sciences (www.NoeticSciences.com) He is quoted as saying, "It is becoming increasingly clear that the human mind and physical universe do not exist independently. Something as yet indefinable connects them. This connective link, between mind and matter, intelligence and intuition, is what Noetic Sciences is about." Noetic is another Greek word. It is a word that was used for 'intuitive knowing.' The Noetic Science Institute focuses on the study of consciousness and human potential.

It is interesting that during the early nineteen hundreds Albert Einstein developed his Theory of Relativity. His theory proved that all things of the universe are interrelated on a molecular level and material things have no boundaries. David Bohm also published on the theory of relativity and quantum physics. Quantum mechanics came next. And later Bohm did work on neuropsychological concepts. All of this has been a little to much for us to comprehend and to realize its significance in our concept of ourselves and the world around us. But Body-Mind medicine (Holistic Health), advanced in the United States by Depak Chopra, M.D., Norman Shealy, M.D., founder of the American Holistic Medical Association, Andrew Weil, M.D., founder of the Foundation for Integrative Medicine, and others has gained wide spread attention today. When we consider the connectedness of our physical world, our thoughts as energy and the intent of our will as creating energy, it leaves open the possibilities for the use of that flow of energy for healing and allowing the mind to reach into areas that would appear totally separate from the physical body.

While certain psychological terminologies have been brought into today's households by science and literature, a working understanding of consciousness has been a part of religion for centuries. The psychological community has brought the religious concepts into their research and they carry the same basic connotation in both systems. And since there is so much already available, I will only give some brief descriptions of consciousness as they pertain to the transcendence process and self healing concepts proposed in this volume.

# Chapter 3

## Simplified Stages of Consciousness

For this purpose, let it be said that when we hold thoughts in the forefront of our minds, we are "aware." But we can also have thoughts running in the background of our actions/activities without being aware of the processing taking place in our sub-conscious mind. When we later "recall" thinking about an earlier thought; that is pulling information from our consciousness into the mind's "awareness." We might say to ourselves, "I remember thinking that I should do that." But, like so much other fleeting information crossing our consciousness, the earlier sub-conscious material becomes 'self-talk' that was not the focus of our minds. That is why we say that it is sub-conscious or un-conscious to us at the time. And whether we are able to bring these thoughts into our awareness determines the amount of our 'consciousnesses'.

A person who functions at a higher degree of consciousness will find it unnecessary to maintain that degree of consciousness at all times to function in the world today. We can do a lot of different things without the need to pay attention to what we are doing. Some of it is called conditioned reflex action and learned behavior. We do these things without thinking about what we are doing. And wouldn't it be difficult if we had to mentally concentrate on EVERY action we took? It is much easier for us to move from one stage to another as the difficulty of our environment dictates.

Consciousness has been grouped into categories, as few as

three to as many as seven. These categories may also include stages of un-consciousness and/or sub-consciousness. For the purpose of our general understanding we will pick three general categories. The first is simple consciousness. The second is self-consciousness. The third is higher-consciousness.

## *Simple Consciousness*

Experimentations on everything from rats to people have pointed to different 'degrees' of consciousness. The lowest form or degree, of consciousness detectable in research is called Simple Consciousness. (There is a body of evidence to suggest consciousness in plants and possibly inanimate objects as well.) Any form of animal, rat to man, who has simple consciousness, is sensual (can react emotionally) and has an intellect (to a limited degree). This degree of consciousness has little or no ability to reason. That is why it is called simple; hence, a person unaware of their surroundings and what is going on is called a simpleton.

## *Self Consciousness*

The second stage of consciousness is Self Consciousness. Self Consciousness reflects the ability of those whom we consider to be 'normal' people in the world today.

Anyone/anything that has attained self-consciousness has the ability to reflect on their own mental state, and to bring thoughts into awareness. Their mind has the ability to think through a series of ideas and/or events and come to an opinion based upon a series of thoughts leading to a conclusion. This is called the ability to reason.

The Self-Conscious mind can become conceptual and imaginative. It can play with ideas.

Thinking in a self-conscious mind can become abstract. Genius is not necessary. But it takes some degree of higher intelligence and discipline than simple consciousness. The discipline may come from the necessity to survive, an interest in learning, or challenges of any nature.

The need to adjust to irregular physical conditions or behavior of another and associated expectations, tend to make the mind more "mindful." Mindful means paying attention to your thoughts and surroundings.

The mind, will, when faced with choices, real or imagined, conceive of the necessary steps, which will often include more than one solution, for the need to win or survive. These 'mind games' are sometimes played out in daydreaming or reverie, but are often times unconsciously formulated. They may also remain unconscious unless the need for them arises.

The Self-Conscious mind can, as a given rule, carry on or follow several activities at a time. (2 to 4 is common) Passive activities of the household (sewing, ironing, cleaning), hobbies (art, crafts, woodworking), monitoring a radio or television show while following the activities of children, and sometimes engaging in conversation with another are examples of parallel activities of the mind. Another might be replaying what happened at work or the grocery store yesterday or imagining or playing out a series of events in your mind that will take place tomorrow.

Only one thought can hold the mind at any one time. But its versatility, flexibility, and resourcefulness (if we could keep up with it) might surprise us. But most of us do not watch our minds unless we are trying to meditate, which is an attempt to quiet the mind instead of tracking it.

When the mind has the capacity to do so, the awareness of things beyond ourselves motivates our exploration of abstract ideas. We may explore literature, religion, and science for ideas that we can contemplate. We may develop a theory or invent something new.

During our lifetime the mind will fluctuate between concentrating on the abstract and conceptual ideas and 'coasting.' This coasting takes place while the mind is engaging life at each moment, or just taking it as it comes. That is because most people prefer a simple routine which does not require them to think about everyday things. Things like chewing food, which keys the fingers will touch while typing, and getting dressed do not take a concentrated effort of thought. Therefore our behavior is most often through habit and simple reflex action/conditioned response. And most of our daily routine of physical activities is handled this way on a daily basis.

The cognitive ability of being self consciousness (versus simple reflex/conditioned response); means becoming introspective, imaginative, self-aware, and self-analytical, with the ability to see alternatives and possibilities. This is, again, abilities of a larger consciousness than the first stage of simple consciousness.

A negative side of this ability to exercise a larger consciousness is that a number of highly intelligent individuals who maintain an elevated state of mental activity nudge against the brink of insanity because of the demands on their minds. Their inability to solve and answer complex questions, and process information which is incomplete, weighs heavily on their mental energies. In other words, they feel something is lacking in their ability to comprehend and communicate with the world around them because of their own higher level of awareness and intelligence.

These same people will have, in many cases, explored several religions and found that none of them answered their questions. They may have looked at societies, governments, and philosophy. If their questions about life cannot be answered to their satisfaction, the mind can break down or the person can become mentally depressed. Also, if religion, per se, which man turns to the most often, does not fully answer the question of the relationship of man to man in a moral, helpful and loving environment, the person can continue to be drawn into self and becomes mentally withdrawn from a society he dislikes and/or cannot comprehend. This is because the concrete, abstract, imaginative mind cannot accept others' stories or faiths. They must have their own answers.

Let me insert here the fact that it is my belief that mental and physical illnesses are caused by chemical reactions in the body. As a result of the body's emotional response to outside factors the body can trigger the biological basis for both mental and physical illness. (I will speak more of 'choices' we make in our reactions to our environment that influence our health.)

For the highly intelligent, self-conscious individual, the thoughts that they may be crazy are common. They come to this conclusion because of their frustration and even anger at life. They feel empty and unfulfilled in spite of their physical and material accomplishments. For them, life is just not working. Their longing and seeking leaves them ever hopeful for something meaningful and satisfying in their lives.

A drink can lead to alcoholism, drugs to addiction, and a sexual encounter may lead to sexual addiction. This is because sexual ecstasy or other addictions is the closest thing to momentary fulfillment they have experienced. After the sexual, or other addictive experience, they keep coming back for more trying to keep the void filled. Most know their lives are out of control, but won't move on unless a relationship becomes abusive or embarrassing, or they recognize there are serious consequences associated with the drugs, alcohol, food, tobacco, etc.

Nevertheless, by sustained observation of thought, and self-examination, man can find a logical, appropriate approach to aspects of life. This should be an important consideration for humanity. This is because all that defines man must also reflect his divine nature. If this aspect of man, his divine nature, is neglected or lost through not being validated or by being belittled, the core of man becomes void and empty. Then, it is said, that the person has lost 'Spirit,' or that 'The spirit has been broken."

A search to fill that void, (whatever degree of void there may be) is what takes us in many directions.

Needless to say, man will seek out enough worthwhile activities and conflicts (chaos through challenging norms, rocking the boat, 'seeking') to bring about true changes in his consciousness, beliefs and attitudes. This behavior can bring him to the knowledge, understanding and wisdom demanded by his Self-Conscious mind for growth.

Often, adversity and self-doubt are the 'springboards' to

human awareness. I believe our behavior and conflicts are chosen by us through divine intervention! (This is 'Soul' working through us!) Out of the chaos that has been created can come the strength and discovery we desire. Since conflicts and crisis are often a forerunner of transcendence, we may move to another level of wisdom and understanding through the experiences we create.

As a conclusion to the growing process we gain insight and strength. This insight and strength promotes the expression of our creativity. Our creativity is an expression of our personal power. Our personal power says we can and we will choose appropriate actions that bring joy to our soul.

## *Higher Consciousness*

We now come to the highest known stage of consciousness. This stage can be known as Universal-consciousness, Cosmic-consciousness, Higher-consciousness, Higher Self, Cosmic Soup, etc. We may or may not have progressed through the chaos. But, our seeking for knowledge and wisdom has created a paradigm shift in our thinking that can open us to accepting our true selves; the 'hu' (God) 'man'. When we speak of our 'Self', we speak of our non-dual self; our at-one-ment with God/Universe. That is to say that we accept the fact that sometime between conception and birth our physical mass is joined with a spiritual essence that we view as an extension of a greater Source. (That source is given many names.) The Source does not put something inside each of us to reflect itself. This Source actually comes to reside within us as individualization-an opportunity for us to be unique. We can only be separated from it by choice.

The separation from God, Our Source, Our Good, our Higher Self, comes through the Ego. Most enlightened persons have little or no ego! Their consciousness tells them that we are all an equal part of the Universe. We are created equal, to be equal. Only the Ego feels the need to judge and put some things (including people) higher, and others lower (to make unequal). But the Enlightened

Ones (and those in the field of Quantum Physics) know that each of our Essence is the same as everything else growing and/or existing on our planet.

Within a spiritual context, anything the Ego does to separate us from God, our true Essence, is called Sin in the religious community.

On the other hand, to connect our Soul/Self with God/Source, Universal/Super Consciousness is to create a pathway for information called Intuition and sometimes, true 'Knowing.' It may also expand our energy systems to accept healing for both ourselves and others. And our connection is not only with our Source, but also with others, nature, and the spiritual realm. When we become a part of the infinite, many aspects of the ego become insignificant and fall away.

Some individuals who enter this stage of consciousness do so through what they call mystical experiences. These are not to be interpreted or confused with paranormal experiences. Mystical experiences are states of awareness that are experienced outside the realm of personal norms for the human race. Examples are thoughts, feelings, and images in the mind, expanded energy and sense of well being that do not have a relevant physical basis. Hence, they are called transpersonal, because they go beyond the physical limitations as we know them.

This larger/higher consciousness seeks knowledge and wisdom beyond our every day existence and bridges the mental evolution of mankind to a cosmic consciousness.

These functions frequently give rise to such questions as to the purpose of life, what is spirit, what is soul? Is the soul immortal? In essence, we become "seekers" in a spiritual sense as a natural conclusion to boredom/confusion in the everyday sense.

Awareness at this stage of evolution also goes beyond the boundaries of one's personal being. Transpersonal Awareness allows thoughts, images, feelings, emotions, and knowledge of the outside world to be assessed through non-physical means. They bring enlightenment to our lives about our lives. When this awareness becomes available to an individual, there is usually a personal transformation and the person takes on higher values. Some choose spiritual paths and practices. But, one cannot remain the same. When we tap into the Universal Mind as Seekers (in a spiritual sense), we experience a fundamental change at the core of our being.

These three levels of consciousness may oversimplify the topic. But the primary reason for the introduction to consciousness is to set a standard for reference. First, where do you place yourself? Level one? Level two? Or level three?

If your spirituality was enhanced by your growth in consciousness would this concept be a worthy consideration? If your Soul's path was more cognizant to you through consciousness, would you sharpen your awareness? Spirituality may have already come knocking if you have had experiences that you dismissed because you thought and feared them to be 'un-natural.' I suggest that any gifts from God and/or the Universe is 'natural' and given for our good and benefit. It is how we use them that can enhance or destroy our lives.

In Fay's Stories, I accepted the information I was being given because no one had told me otherwise (one of the advantages of living on the perimeters of my family, and later, society).

When you read Fay's stories, you will also see how my intuition and 'knowing' created a synergy in my life. And how the synchronicity created by it kept telling me that I was on the right tract.

This was brought to my attention by what I called 'mini-miracles' (meaning small). Not that one miracle is any bigger nor smaller than another, but because I was able to recognize the small ways which they affected my life. They were little bits of "goodness" being created in my life. It was as if a path was created for me to keep moving forward.

## There is More

If you had to put into words your formula, or philosophy, of life…..how would you define it?

Somewhere along the way you have developed an individual method of handling life's situations. Very often we hear the "poor me" attitude. Sometimes it's the "you can't get to me" approach. Or, "you leave me alone and I will leave you alone." And for others, how about, "I can't win for losing." "I knew it was going to turn out wrong!"

It seems that as life provides us with worthwhile experiences the outcome becomes interpreted negatively. And the formulas we use for survival causes us to gradually lose our personal power. As a result we become angry and unforgiving. These formulas may have been taught to us by parents, friends and well meaning others. Or, like most of us, we are never taught anything about life; probably because few people will take a stand as to what life is all about. And if they do, it is usually so lofty religiously speaking, that as children we cannot relate to it. By the time we become adults everyone assumes we have it figured out.

Most would agree that we can experience life more fully when we are physically, mentally and emotionally healthy. Then, the question is, "How do we develop and maintain healthiness?" Or how do you optimize the level of health you presently maintain?

I suggest that we can open ourselves to becoming more than

what our physical self and concrete minds allow! We can have a shift in consciousness. We can create a personal power that will enrich our lives by recognizing the choices we are making. When we are aware of the process of living, and we can recognize the synergy created by our choices, our lives can become happier, more fulfilled and healthier.

The Stories of Fay that follow are entertaining and informative. But, more than anything, they tell the story of my deprivation and the trauma that was overcome by my realization that I always had choices, and ultimately it was my decision to follow my consciousness and the path my Soul was showing me as I responded to life, and chose the life I would live. This gave me the personal power not only to survive but also to succeed.

# PART II

# *Deprivation*

"Stories of Fay"

# Sea glass
## - Cranberry Island

*You wanderer of shores unknown;*
*A thing of beauty glistening in the sun.*
*With ragged edges shaped by waves of life.*
*Broken and smoothed, cracked and chipped,*
*Indented with mishaps of turmoil and strife,*
*And polished with smooth rippling water and sand.*
*Translucent, yet opaque to man.*

*Where are the parts of you that you left behind?*
*Are you complete in what remain? Maybe once*
*Round and plump, you now lie flat and thin*
*And made of substance firm, compressed.*
*I look at you and see bubbles of laughter rising*
*From within you. You are my inspiration.*

~ Zalora Price ~

# Prelude

# Prelude

The following memoirs are flashes of memory from/during the first nineteen years of my life.

I would like to repeat – the stories are not about my life. That is another book! They are chosen stories about 'my self awareness' as I am faced with hardship. They are a look at prolonged deprivation in my life in the areas of physical, emotional, social, educational and spiritual neglect, and my response to it.

My intent is to focus on my awareness. In doing so, I am hoping that the reader can relate (not to the circumstances but) to my consciousness and thought processes, that could assist one in becoming more aware of conditions and circumstances in their own lives.

But awareness is not enough. Action is required. I have given the steps I took in Part Three as a twelve step process. By following my heart/soul I survived. By healing I became the person I was meant to be.

For those who wish to 'grow' may your consciousness/awareness take you from the circumstances and/or survival to understanding and growth, and a healthier, happier you.

# 1

## The Spirit Has Landed

**Date**: March 10, 1940
**Place** Pole Road.
Between Clarkton and Gideon, Missouri

*"Throw her in the ditch. I don't want her."*

Winter skies grayed the sunset about 4:00 PM as a small, frail woman prepared for childbirth inside a teepee style canvas tent. It was sitting off the main road, on the bank of a large drainage ditch. A small wood stove sat in the middle of the room, and the stovepipe extended through the center hole of the roof. The bed was placed close to the wall. A homemade table and a chair with a rawhide seat sat close to the flap opening. Two large tin cans, normally purchased with fifty pounds of lard, sit close by. They now held only a small quantity of lard and flour between them, and were also used as make shift chairs. A few rabbit and squirrel hides hung on the walls drying where many more would normally have been. With game for trapping and hunting disappearing from the area it had been several weeks since a proper meal had been put on the table. Of late the woman's diet had most recently consisted of wild turnips pulled from the fields and tea brewed from the dug up roots of a sassafras tree.

This would be the fourth birth for Addie Johnson, but circumstances were more difficult this time. She and her sister had been giving blood every other day to her hospitalized six year old, second child, Estelle, who was to die a month later.

Frances, the oldest, was eight years old. Jim, the third child was only two and a half. They had left earlier in the day for an hour walk to the home of their grandparents.

Two neighbors, hearing of the forth-coming event, had arrived and sat themselves down next to the doorway to chat.

Labor had become intense. And the long hours of contractions had left Addie weak. Her breathing came in short breaths. In spite of the canvas tent and the winter day, her short, auburn hair lay in ringlets around her wet face. Her cotton dress was soaked with perspiration.

A rubber sheet had been placed on top of the uneven straw mattress. A pocket of blood was accumulating between her legs. With a scream and what could have easily been her last breath, her small infant slipped out, face down, into the enlarged puddle of blood. The brilliant red hair was evident in spite of the wetness and the blood streaked head. Her small frame wiggled and a gurgle arose from her face on the bottom of the pool of blood.

Addie lay there, weak from exhaustion. She tried to reach her baby. But she could not move the limp limbs of her own body.
"Please help me." she spoke, barely above a whisper.
"Please."
The two women, sitting only two feet away, stared toward the bed. Neither moved.

At that moment another figure burst through the doorway. She appeared to be an unlikely person to be of any help. Standing

## Deprivation Trauma

there with short, tightly curled hair, red lips and plucked eyebrows, a loose woman like her looked out of place with the other homely females. She surveyed the situation, and quickly realized that Addie was in need and the others were too frightened at the sight of the blood to help.

With barely a moments pause she walked quickly to the bed. "Get me some hot water and a knife." She said.

The two other females immediately jumped from their paralyzed positions and began to follow orders. She lifted the baby from the blood and held it upside down. Blood and mucus streamed from its nose and mouth. A moment later she slapped the baby on the buttocks. With a gasp of air into its lungs the infant whaled.

Minutes later the cord was cut and tied, the baby cleaned, and wrapped in a piece of cotton material from a laundered flour sack. It was obvious that nothing more was available for covering the child.

She then attended to the mother.

Smiling to the frail figure on the bed, the woman left as abruptly as she had entered.

It was beginning to get dark when the uninvited guest had finished with the mother and baby.

She hurried back to her own home. It was a simple three room shot-gun style, wood frame, house. But she knew it would be warm and cozy with its floral wallpaper and curtains on the windows.

She went immediately to the bedroom in the back. Lifting a box from under the bed, she gently placed it on top of the heavy handmade quilt on the bed.

There was a tinge of pain and her eyes were misty as she began to feel the soft pieces of the layette. Each piece had been folded carefully when it was put away, just as she had carefully and lovingly sewn each piece awaiting the arrival of her own child. No one had been there for her. Not someone like her! Her baby had died.

Without further hesitation, she lifted the box and entered the darkness to return to the tent dwelling.

She stayed only long enough to check the mother and infant.
Placing the box within reach, she opened it slowly showing the tiny gowns, navel bands, and diapers.
Again, she left.
Her name was Fay. (My namesake.)


It had started to hail by late evening when the two older children returned. The hail pounded on the tiny tent. The roof swayed with its weight. The doorway had to be cleared for their entry.

Both stood by the bed, urgently awaiting the news. "Jim," mother said, "You have a baby sister." Turning abruptly, with unshielded anger, he replied, "Throw her in the ditch. I don't want her."

# Chapter 2

## From the Minds of Babes

> *I knew and completely understood the essence of those around me.*

The question which arises is, "At what age does a being acquire consciousness?" Also, how does that consciousness and the degree of that consciousness effectively influence the remainder of our lives? Must we have memory to prove consciousness? Would you believe me, if I told you that I remember things from birth?

Reasoning deductively, my consciousness at birth was definitely in place. I cannot prove to you the pictures in my mind. I do not recall understanding the words being spoken. But they were not necessary. I KNEW and completely understood the essence of those around me. I knew my mother carried me with indifference, and at times with anger and hatred. My father cared for children but never seemed to be totally connected to life. He could love me without ever feeling a total responsibility towards my health and safety; which a child must depend on from parents.

My basic care was passed on to my older sister. She was only eight years old. She treated me like a doll. She would hold me close and do anything she could for me with her limited resources. She had such a sweet spirit and because I felt safer with her I cried little.

Long periods of time seemed to elapse as I spent hours upon

hours alone on my pallet near home or at the end of the rows of cotton in the fields. There seemed to be a rush to set me aside so the others could get on with their lives. What little care I received was done without any direct attention towards me. The nonverbal message was to stay out of the way and do not make any demands. I learned that most often no one would be there. If someone were to be there I would simply be ignored.

Spending so much time alone I would watch the actions of those around me. I remember the constant wonder I had at the actions of my family. Their behavior amused me. At times I considered their behavior ridiculous and without reason. I felt, surely, that I was in the wrong family, because they never reasoned or thought the same as I did.

At birth the spiritual essence within me felt the same size as the adults in my family and I felt equal to them. I sensed that the path (lives) of my mother, father, sisters, and brothers had something to do with me on a spiritual (soul/consciousness) level because I was practicing (patience) before I could verbally communicate with them. It was simply a 'knowing' that if I were to learn from them I had to be patient. But at the time, from the information I got from them, there was so much I did not understand or at least accept as my truth. I knew I had to find a way to bridge the gap between us, and all the other people I expected to come into my life.

First and foremost, I understood that I was a spiritual being on a physical journey. Maybe I did not think of it in that way. But when I thought of myself I thought of myself being inside the body I was in and not as the body itself. Since I felt the same size as the adults it was difficult to handle their attitude and treatment of me. As I watched my body grow, and attempted to understand my family in the years that followed, the discourse between us brought to me a sense of endurance. I knew that if 'I' were to survive that my 'body' had to survive. I knew my family was a part of my experience on earth with all its difficulties and confusion.

This somehow made it alright for them to be who they were and for me to be who I was. And I struggled against their attitudes toward life that reinforced concepts in my mind that I did not feel were the true reality of things.

It seemed that deep within my 'knowing' that relationships were to be a focus in my life and I was off to a difficult start.

Because of my age and small size, I did not dare get involved in a verbal or reasoning conflict with my family even after I learned how to communicate with them. I listened while they seemed to always be in judgment of something or someone. While they criticized, I made excuses for others and their circumstances in my mind. My family was so narrow-minded. Why couldn't they see the whole picture? Where was their understanding?

There was much I knew without asking, and I never got the answers I wanted when I did ask (looking for validation). I had to develop more and more patience trying to understand. And when I found I could not understand them and had difficulty coping with their behavior, then I could only return to love and accept them as different from me.

During those early years (1-7 years), I learned to keep my thoughts and feelings to myself. To survive the outburst of anger and resentment I found it necessary to became reserved and somewhat withdrawn.

By the time I arrived, Dad had pretty much walked out on us as a provider. But, occasionally, Mother came to his rescue by telling the story of when Grandpa became drunk and hit Dad across the head with a piece of firewood. "He has never been the same," she would say.

Whatever drove my mother drove her hard. And she took my brother Jim with her. Maybe their relationship was based upon Karma. Maybe it was circumstances. But there was an extreme closeness between them. From the very beginning, either their relationship had no room for others or they both simply did not want me in their lives. It only grew stronger with years. He was her 'favorite.' And they were separated from me by their own choosing. Over time, I understood it had nothing to do with me as a person. They had their own path.

I was four years old when mother had another child, which she did not want and would not care for. Even though I had questioned their behavior towards me, it was then that I knew for certain that my rejection and abandonment had nothing to do with me personally. But that knowledge did not lessen my loneliness and need for adult care. And out of necessity, I remained alone, detached, and self-sufficient.

My mother's pregnancy and the birth of my sister fired an anger and violence towards me beyond what I had already experienced. In a world of my own, I turned to dreaming or dreading! And a lot of it was planning; planning on how I could survive. I was helpless. So, my best tools were to be passive and as 'unseen' as possible.

My brother, Jim, was quick to hurt me, and also often followed Mother's attacks with a verbal reminder and a physical blow to remind me that I was to stay out of their lives. This further validated my feelings that I was not a part of this family. A part of me certainly did not want to be there. Another part of me could not understand why I was there and why I had to stand alone, and watch the rest of the people live their lives around me.

In my attempt to understand and a realization that came one day, an experience has remained with me since the age of three. I remember relatives coming for a visit. There were adults and children. The children were told to go into the yard and play. I remained seated with my hands folded in my lap. (This was my passive posture.)

My mother, hoping to sound nice, said to me, "Fay, why don't you go out and play with the others?" I had already surveyed the situation and I shook my head. I knew what to expect from other children after living with my brother for three years. All the children were within two years of me. If each of them hit me just once, I would not be able to get up or may not survive the attack. I could not put my body in harms way. On the other hand, by listening to the adults, maybe I could learn more about older people and lives beyond the confines of my existence. Maybe I could understand more.

But I soon concluded (my exact thought) "that they didn't know much about anything." Everything they had to say was idle chatter. I was disappointed. There was more to life and I wanted to know what it was. How could I get there? How long would I have to wait?

# Chapter 3

## Continuity of Life

> *Did our Soul choose to come into this 'life' to do something or to learn something?*

It is a common belief that life is a continuum. It is widely held that there is spiritual life after the death of our physical bodies. Some hold that there is a spiritual life BEFORE this physical journey, and we will transition BACK to spirit after this physical existence ends. If the latter is true, maybe there has been too much emphasis on the afterlife (transition back) from our religious systems, and not enough on our choice and reason(s) for this incarnation on earth. Did our Soul choose to come into this 'life' to do something or to learn something? Or were we forced to be here for punishment?

My first reasoning as a child was that I had been sent here to be punished. That was why life was so difficult! When I heard the words 'heaven' and 'hell' in my grandmother's church service at the age of ten, I thought that if 'heaven' was 'up' there, then, for certain I was 'down' in 'hell' on earth.

So much research has been done on physical growth and development from birth to death. Why has our spirit been so neglected?

The neglect may be because there is no standardized way to document the working of spirit in our lives. Lack of scientific evidence does not mean it does not exist. It simply means that technologies and instruments, and research techniques must be developed for that purpose. And personal studies can be done. But, more importantly, our culture must grow in self-awareness and encourage this research for publication. Religion, as an institution, should examine its role in nurturing the Spirit as a spirit, and not as a body.

Much is being said today about the creative power of the mind and its dominion over all conditions of life and the body. This is good; because it takes us to the next step of realizing that when the mind works in harmony with our higher self (innate intelligence/ wisdom) we become more aware of our soul path.

Nobody told me I had a soul path. I think when I became convinced that I had entered this earth form as a fully conscious being, it seemed logical to me that I had incarnated (my spirit born into a human body) for a reason, and maybe a purpose. I was also aware that sometimes things happened to me, in spite of everything I could do to prevent the incidents. If I could not control things, maybe those things were necessary, for me to learn something in this life.

Sometimes certain things did not happen, in spite of everything I tried to do to MAKE them happen. Following anger and frustration, a form of awareness developed; an awareness that says someone or something else is in control....a God-force, if you wish. By my teens, I had come to recognize that when I paid attention and looked at the overall picture, that this force – power – energy, had my 'good' in mind. And when I could trust this higher force to serve my best good, then I could 'let go and let god' or let the 'universal energy' flow in my life. Then tremendous peace would follow. I could tune in to the energy source that spoke to my mind through my body. The habit of continually checking with my inner self kept me on track towards life's goals.

My eyes and external reality told me many things that went contrary to my 'gut' feelings. So, I went 'checking' very often. And I chose to follow the leading of my inner-guide (innate intelligence) over the external appearances. I developed a 'yes,' 'no' communication system with my Innate, God Source, Universal Energy, Infinite Mind, Cosmic Soup, whatever you want to call it. There was a definite 'yes' or 'no' response from my body that told me to proceed, or to wait. This is right. This is wrong. This response system became my reality. But, since my life was simple and I had to make few major choices, the system was used most often in my relationships and interactions with other people.

As a newborn and young child, my whole world seemed wrong. Everything went contrary to my nature. I wanted to be loved and to give love. Instead, I was treated with anger and hatred. I wanted food and attention. I was starved and ignored. I wanted to be validated as belonging and having some sense of worth. I was to learn that my family of origin and the outside community were quick to reject me and to ridicule me, without mercy. My inner dialogue countered every attack with wisdom and patience. I observed the world with wonder and silence. I knew I could not teach them what they did not want to know.

# Chapter 4

## Joining the Family

> *The need for survival broadened my senses.*

For all practical purposes, I was simply ignored within the family. When it was necessary to communicate with me, I was yelled AT. Never, in my childhood, can I remember EVER being talked WITH. It came to be in my best interest to NOT be seen or heard. When Mother became angry, which she often was, she liked to beat on the child that was available to her, excluding my brother, Jim. That meant me, for a reason I never knew. There was Frances. She was Mother's first born, and she and Estelle were from her first marriage. Maybe my arrival made her life too complicated.

During the first four years of my life I was drawn to her because I felt her pain, which was causing her the frustration and anger. I wanted to help, to comfort her. Instead I bore the brunt of her volatile emotions.

In the wintertime it was usually the slaps across the face that sent me sailing to the other side of the room. When I cried, she would yell at me to "Shut-up!" And she would continue to beat me until I could hold my sobs. On other occasions she would shake me until I was dizzy and dulled.

In the summertime she liked to go to the yard for a peach tree limb or a willow branch. She would raise and/or lower my clothing and whip me until she could see the blood welling up on my skin. And at times, she got so carried away that she did not stop soon enough and the blood would run down my back and legs. She always seemed to be exhausted after a beating and much calmer. I think I continued to be near her for a period of time because I felt I was helping. But at the age of three and four, I was also feeling anger and my own pain.

Nothing in my life 'seemed' right. No one came to me when I was hurting. No one cared if I was sad, hungry, or ill. Offering myself as a sacrificial lamb to my mother brought me nothing in return.

I tried to stay clear of all adults. And when forced into their presence, I remained silent and unobtrusive. I entered a world of aloneness and mental isolation; developing an acute sense of awareness. I was like a small animal seeking and sneaking for survival in a hostile environment. Always alert, always ready for retreat. I stood behind a camouflage of anything available.

The need for survival broadened my senses. From behind closed doors I could sense movement, footsteps, and breathing. I would know someone was in the room or in the yard, and know what they were doing. Even at night, I became aware of movement in the airspace around me and could tell if someone was near or moving several feet away. I became a "light sleeper."

By the age of three I had expanded my energy space to surround me at some distance. When that space was invaded, all my senses became alert. Initially my comfort zone/personal space was only a few feet around me. But when I would get slapped for no obvious reason, I would back away at a greater distance, hoping not to be within reach of an angry hand. Then there was a hand holding a board, a piece of firewood, or something else available. Each time I physically and psychologically moved back, my energy field would expand.

A memory during this time stands out in my mind. It tells the story of my young years because it is indicative of many such memories of difficult times and treatments.

I was three. Just three! It was cold. So cold. My daddy was gone to be in the War and my sister was not yet born. It was the early winter months of 1943. I remember a lot of people in our house. Seems they were always there…talking, smoking, drinking coffee, and playing cards, until long past my bedtime; which was anytime I chose to crawl under a dirty quilt. Nobody cared or noticed.

That particular evening my stomach ached from hunger. I complained again and again, hoping for something to eat. I eventually tired and went to bed. But I could not sleep because of the pain in my stomach. I went back to the adults at the card table. When I disturbed them again, I was severely scolded and threatened with a whipping if I did not leave them alone. Because, as my mother repeated, there was nothing to eat.

As I raised my head to the table above me, I could see coffee cups and cigarette smoke curling in the air above their heads. It was obvious to me that the adults had money for cigarettes and coffee for themselves. But, they had no money for food for me.

Jim had been gone with Mother all day. I knew they had eaten. Why couldn't I eat? I knew. They did not want me. They did not want me to eat their food. They did not want to acknowledge my existence. To recognize me as a person, being with them meant giving me some consideration. They did not want me. They had never wanted me. And even now, they refused me the basic essentials of life. The mere tangibles! Oh, what a little of the intangibles could have done for me also! Any small expressions of love or concern!!!

The cards, coffee, and cigarettes became objects of disgust, disrespect, and suspicion. And later, there was shame attached to my mother's cigarette smoking, knowing that her addiction to tobacco overrode any other consideration in her life; and knowing that my life and health came second to her coffee and cigarettes. Any given memory of my childhood includes the feelings of hunger and cold, and the memory of cigarettes and coffee.

# Chapter 5

## Opposites Attract

> *The extreme differences between them left few possibilities for mutual benefit.*

My father was in the household during the years I was living with my family. But I never felt I knew him. I knew he was a good man. A kind man. A caring man. A quiet man. A person who never seemed to comprehend his environment except in the woods and on the river. He could be alone with himself and with nature. People seemed to confuse him. The only pleasurable interaction he seemed to derive was through taking an opposite stand on most anything my mother stated as true. I don't think I ever heard him come up with an original idea in their disagreements. It was a matter of him turning around something she had said. The hours of arguing made me very uncomfortable and over the years came to upset me greatly. I vowed I would never argue with my spouse.

Something I sensed rather than knew about my father was his spiritual self. I could not explain it as a child or as a young adult, but when I came to be in his presence there was a comforting feeling; a 'knowing' that permeated my being and generated a sense of closeness and lovingness. In his own nonverbal way he taught me to grow calm, serene, and gentle.

I think he loved my mother. The extreme differences between them left little possibilities for mutual benefit within the marriage. I often times thought the arguing was the only time he could tie her down to giving him her undivided time and attention.

I heard it said he was a 'dreamer.' That seemed to mean two things to me. He talked often about things that were going to happen in the world. Most of the things seemed to be biblical or politically based. The other was his ability to spend so much time doing nothing physical. His idea of providing a living for his family was sitting in the boat all day waiting for the fish to bite or running his trotlines or traps every few days…which could spread into many days if it was too hot, too cold, too windy, too dry, too far to walk, too far to carry them, etc., etc. I cannot say that my father was lazy. It seemed to be more of a lack of intensity. And my mother had more than enough intensity for both! Her intensity paved the way (gave me an example to follow) for my own early physical survival, and his spiritual example validated my spiritual side.

# 6

## Life Gets Worse

August - 1943

> *For the next four months he did unbelievable things.*

I had just turned three years of age in 1943 when my dad was called to active duty in the U.S. Army for World War II. We were living out in the country between Marked Tree and Lepanto, Arkansas. Dad had been gone a few months, and Mother had started to spend time in bed. The four room wood frame house with its large front porch still stands out in my mind. There were the cotton, corn, and soybean fields growing right up to the yard, and the woodland in back.

That summer, large trucks with German prisoners of war would stop in front of our house. Our house was far back from the main road, sandwiched between the woods and the fields. The 'road' was a gumbo mud trail leading to our house. But in the summer heat, the mud ruts were dry and bumpy, but passable. Soldiers with rifles would watch the prisoner as they worked in the fields.

There was one young officer who spent a lot of time with my mother. His skin was very white, and his hair was the blackest I had ever seen. His eyes were a pure, unusual green. I was young and he didn't seem to mind that I saw him holding Mother's hand when he came to see her and found her in her bed.

In a few weeks the crops were harvested. Mother decided to move us to Missouri. We lived near Clarkton, Missouri until after my sister was born in April, 1944.

Marked Tree, Arkansas - 1944

After my sister's birth, Mother found a large farm house and moved us back to Arkansas. Her younger sister and common law husband, Frank, and their daughter, moved in with us to help share in the expenses. Aunt Carrie did the cooking and looked after the house and kids. Mother, with Jim in tow, worked in the fields.

It should have been a good arrangement. But somewhere along the way, Frank had decided to bring along a hand gun. Secretly, to Aunt Carrie, he threatened to kill everyone if she did not keep quite about the gun. He made her sew a special pocket in his coat for the gun so no one would know that he had it.

I can only suppose that when the excitement wore off on having the gun and making his threats, he decided he could take things a step further. And for the next four months he did unbelievable things. His daughter and I were four. My cousin and aunt (Mom's youngest sister) were six. Nancy was only four months old. Fran was twelve, almost thirteen.

It started one morning.

"Frances, wake up."

"Hum-m-m."

Carrie's voice was quiet, but had a quality that caused Fran to lower the quilt from her head and blink her eyes. It was a summer day and the sun shining through the barren window had just taken the chill from the room. There were two of them in the room. Carrie stood by the bed. A few feet away stood Frank, her husband.

"He wants to do 'it' to you today."

I raised my head also. Realizing it was morning; I threw back the covers and started to crawl out over the quilts.

"Fay!" "Lay back down. Cover your head." Aunt Carrie

said strongly.

Puzzled, but obedient, I lay back down. And wrapping the warm blankets around myself, I listened to the muffled voices.

"He wants you on the edge of the bed." Carrie said.

Fran cautiously, and a bit frightened, moved to the end of the bed and sat on the edge. Placing her hand on Fran's shoulder, Carrie slowly pressed Fran backward until she was laying flat on her back with her legs hanging from the bed.

Frank moved in front of her and reached for her panties. The bed rocked as she protested. She knew what 'it' was. Frightened, she looked to her aunt. Carrie assured her that it would not take long and she was there with her.

Raising her legs and pulling them around his body, Frank leaned into Frances until her buttocks rested on his pelvis. Holding her with one hand around the waist, the other hand moved between her legs. Then he put his finger into her vagina. Startled and uncomfortable, she flinched and tightened her vaginal muscles as if to expel the intrusion. Noting her resistance, he decided to proceed quickly with this first encounter. Placing his penis between her legs, he pushed himself into her. Gasping with the unexpected pain, Frances moans and struggled to back herself away from him. Holding Fran with her left hand so she could not move, Carrie placed her right hand over Fran's mouth to stifle the almost childlike sounds that were mounting in shrillness and intensity. A few more jerks, and he pulled away from her.

Carrie spoke softly again, "Come with me and I will clean you up. Then you can go back to bed."

"But, he wants to do it again today."

Where was everybody? Fran walked through the house and into the back yard. The car was gone. So were Mother and Jim. They would be gone all day. She knew, and 'they' also knew. Plenty of time to do whatever they wanted to do.

Turning to me, she said, "Fay, you'd better play way out in the back today. They might want to do "it" to you too. Better stay gone until Mom gets back."

I loved being in the sunshine. The sunlight energized me. And being alone for the day was nothing new for me. I made my way into the woods that surrounded our house on the left side and around the back. The trees were tall, and mostly red and black oak. There were a few maple and sweet gum. All of them provided a nice canopy, and even some lower branches hung low enough for me to climb. In that eastern stretch of the Ozark Mountain range, there was little undergrowth, but lots of places for a little one to hide.

I did not know what time it was. But I was hungry. I realized that I had left the house without eating anything that morning. I looked around me. There was always some sheepshank growing along the edge of the woodland. I liked its tangy taste. But, it wasn't filling. I looked for some nut grass. Then I remembered that it only grew around the fields where the land had been cultivated. I wasn't sure about the mushrooms growing around the trees. I had been warned that some of them were poisonous. There may have been some papaws still growing, but the trees I found had none.

By the sun, I knew it was mid-afternoon when I returned to the yard. Frances was stirring the clothes inside the large black iron kettle over the fire in the yard. Standing back from the coals, she leaned over stirring the mixture of lye soap, boiling water, and sheets with a wooden paddle cut for that purpose. I slowly approached the kettle. "I'm hungry." I said.

"We'll see if we can find something." Fran replied.

As we turned towards the back door, it opened. "Fran, he is ready for you again. He wants you against that wall." Carrie and Frank both stood in the doorway. As Carrie stepped forward to take Fran's reluctant hand, she whispered quickly to me, "Don't stay! Go!"

## Deprivation Trauma

It was probably two weeks later. I was in the kitchen with Nancy and Aunt Carrie. Aunt Carrie was standing across from us cleaning up after breakfast. She had started to wash some dishes.

Nancy was sitting in her highchair. My head came almost to her tray. When she would fuss or cry, I would give her some attention while Aunt Carrie continued her chores at the sink. But Nancy was becoming very fretful because it was time for her bottle. Aunt Carrie eventually put a bottle of milk in a pan of water on the stove. By that time I was having no success in distracting her from her hunger.

Frank came into the room. I had not heard him enter. When I looked up, he was moving his body against Nancy's chair. His hand was directing his penis towards her mouth. He placed it against her lips. Her small tongue came out searching for the nipple of her bottle. It moved rapidly about the penis and I saw the penis become larger. She fussed ever louder when her lips could not grasp the object. Aunt Carrie turned. "Don't do that to the baby." She said.

He laughed. "She likes it." He said.

"She wants her bottle." She replied, putting a stern look on her face to show him that she really did not like what he was doing.

Nancy's impatience became full blown anger. Her mouth opened wide with her screams. With her mouth open wide, he slid his penis between her pink gums. Immediately she began to suck and pull at his penis trying to receive the nourishment she craved. In only seconds, he began to move, pushing and pulling against her resistance. She, then, opened her mouth to scream, in resistance, to the false intrusion. But, doing so, she allowed him to push himself further into her mouth. To this, she gagged. He pushed in and out, pushing harder and harder against the back of her throat. Then the gagging stopped. I heard a gurgle escape from her before her breathing was shut off entirely. Her face began to turn red. Her whole face and neck were red. Aunt Carrie ran to the highchair. "Stop it," she screamed. She was pulling at him wildly as he fought her off. "You are going to hurt her." She pulled at him. Nancy was turning blue. He was holding on to the baby, while trying in a wild frenzy to reach orgasm. It seemed to be played out in slow motion before my eyes. I saw her tiny mouth stretched until it looked like it would tear. Her soft white skin turned red. Then it turned blue and her tiny body trembled. When he pulled away, her body was limp and lifeless. Carrie shook Nancy. There was no response. Her fingers worked quickly to remove the straps holding her in the chair. She was no longer crying. She was not making any sound. I watched as she shook Nancy. She threw Nancy over her shoulder and patted her sharply on the back as she walked anxiously back and forth between the table and sink. She was talking to Nancy and to herself. Then she held Nancy away from her and firmly struck her between her shoulders. Nancy began to cry and her whole body gave a prolonged shudder. Carrie held her to her breast and tried to quiet her. Nothing worked until her bottle was placed to her mouth. She sucked almost violently, as if to satiate the trauma she had just experienced.

I consciously found myself planted to the kitchen floor. I was holding my breath as I watched in horror and fear. Only when Nancy breathed again was I able to inhale again. And when I tried to swallow, I found that my mouth was open and my lower jaw muscles were clenched and resistant to movement. My body was a mirror to her pain. I had felt the suffocation and fear. I sneaked away, fearful that the same could happen to me. It never did.

Two months later, the six of us girls were taken to the doctor's office. I was the only one who had not been sexually abused. I was the only one who left the office without "treatment". The others had gonorrhea. Nancy was six months old!

I think only one thing saved me from being 'sexually' (as being separate from psychologically) abused. I was my grandfather's favorite grandchild. That was because I was the first child in the family to be born with red hair, which brought out our Irish heritage. And my grandfather was also a Marshall, and maybe the best man with a gun, in those parts.

Seeing Nancy's assault haunted me from that day onward. Anytime I put a toothbrush into my mouth, or a large piece of food, I would start gagging and having difficulty getting my breath, and at times becoming weak and ill. I began to cut my food in tiny pieces, and chewing and chewing, so I would not start gagging when I tried to swallow. I had difficulty with eating for several years. I was not concerned about grabbing for some share of food from our table for that reason and it contributed to my malnutrition. And all the talk about sex among teenagers left me feeling tense, uneasy, and afraid. Plus, the feeling of helplessness I felt during the experiences with both Frances and Nancy came back to haunt me.

# From County to Town

1944 – Apartment, Lepanto, Arkansas

> *If we could protect children from unhealthy conditions, they would not have the extent of physical, mental, and emotional problems they face today from the trauma.*

Our move into an apartment in town was the best we could do when Aunt Carrie and Frank, and Carrie Ann secretly left our home in the country. After our trip to the doctor, there was probably no doubt in Frank's mind that Mother would be returning with a sheriff. And he was right. After everything that was happening in Mother's life, this only served to fuel her anger. If he had not been gone, I think she would have found a way to kill him.

I do not remember the apartment very well. I have a vision of the bed Mom and I slept on, which was by the front door. My side of the bed was in the corner. I could see from there into the kitchen in the back. The two rooms seemed to be the lower area of a larger building and could have been a storage area at some time.

The ceilings were low and there was only one window in the whole apartment. It was located on the other end of the apartment at the back of the kitchen. The place was very dark.

We had not been there longer than two weeks when we went to bed one night. Nancy had a crib and Fran and Jim slept on rollaway type beds. We all slept in the same room.

It seems like we had only been asleep a while when I awoke with a stinging pain in my left groin. The pain was intense. I was whimpering but afraid to wake my mother. She became irritated as the pain became worse and my reaction became louder. She reached in the dark and found a wood match stick and lit the oil lamp. Angrily, she threw back the covers to see where I hurt. There, on the bed sheet beside me, was a black spider. It had a shiny body with a red hourglass design on its back. Mother took the match stick she had used for lighting the lamp and tried to move it away from me. It reared on its back legs and fought with her. The last thing I remember was her trying to get it off the bed to kill it.

I was awake. I couldn't open my eyes. My body did not want to move either. I lay there. Then, I heard murmurs. Voices far away. I dozed off.

When I awoke again, I could move my head. I could see through a thin slit in my eye lids. But not well. There were several people in that small room. Mother's voice came to me first. "She's awake".

Someone was sitting on the bed beside me. A man. "Her fever has broken," he was saying. "She will live."

I could hear exhausted sighs of relief. Someone raised my head and put a glass of water to my lips. "Keep her quiet for a few days," he said.

## Deprivation Trauma

The story was told to me over and over. It was told, mostly, out of wonderment. Mother had sat up with me for two days and two nights. The small town doctor had been there too, most of the time. Seems I began to turn dark from my shoulders down to my knees, and also quickly became delirious. Mother ran to the doctor's house which was only three blocks away. It only took him minutes to get there. But I was already out. His only assurance was that if they could keep me alive until my fever broke, I would make it. So they sat over me, sponging me with cold water.

We moved out of the dark, dank, mildewing apartment. And I have always looked for Black Widow spiders in any dark space.

Whether it is insects, rodents, scorpions, spiders, or any other dangerous or unclean creature in the home environment, children always seem most at risk. I think our society depends too much upon the medical profession to spend its time repairing broken bodies and minds, after the damage is done. If we could protect children from unhealthy conditions, they would not have the extent of physical, mental, and emotional problems that they face from the trauma.

# 8

## I Didn't Know I Could Not Fly

It was spring, 1945.

> *We reject, eliminate, deny, and forget about our greatest potential; simply because someone tells us it is not within our grasp.*

Mother had moved us into another apartment. Lepanto, Arkansas was a very small town. But living conditions were better than in the country, even though the apartments in town were small.

We had walked to the local store for some items. This was an exciting experience for me, since I had no concept of what a 'store' would look like and the things that would be on display.

I felt very shy and reluctant to leave my mother's side. But she put me in the middle of the store and instructed me to remain there. The store was about fourteen feet wide by twenty feet deep. It had a meat counter with a glass front sitting near the door. Beyond it sat large tin cans of lard, flour, beans, and roots. There were a few canned goods and miscellaneous items on a shelf in the back. A pot belly wood stove sat to the other side of the store and some men sat around it talking.

I could remember very little about my father. But I knew I

had a father and that he was in the Army. I looked at the men wondering if my father was like one of them. When they returned my look, I shied away and pressed myself against the nearby glass food case filled with meats and cheeses. They each wore blue denim overalls and various colors of plaid flannel shirts. Two had a small can that they shared as they handed it back and forth spitting tobacco juice into it. Their high topped shoes stretched out towards the stove showed their rolled-down cotton socks. One wore a high topped cap that I later came to recognize as a train engineer's hat. I waited there for my mother to finish shopping.

I was anxious to leave the store, and actually ran ahead of my older sister and my mother, (who was carrying my baby sister) when we left the store. It seemed to be the most beautiful day of my life. The sun was warm. Everything was green and the birds were singing. As I hurried along, following the sound of birds in the trees, I felt myself rise off the sidewalk. I continued about one foot above the walk for a distance. "What fun," I thought. "I must tell my mother that I have done something new!" (I was always trying to find ways to please her.) I ran back to find her. I called to her before I reached her. "Mommy, I flew. I can fly!"

Without breaking her pace or looking my way, she responded, "People do not fly. Don't lie to me again."

I did not understand; only that I was not to speak of it again.

Had I known that people do not fly, would I have lifted off the ground that beautiful day to soar with the birds? Probably not! But in many areas of our lives we accept only the 'acceptable.' And we reject, eliminate, deny, and forget about our greatest potential- simply because someone tells us it is not within our grasp.

The ideas are communicated to us in many shapes and forms. Society has a way with words, attitudes, and expectations. For the poor, the minority, the disabled, and for others, the challenge is consistently with us.

The expectation is for us to conform, to be like others. And in many cases that means that we are to uphold the beliefs and values, and remain within the group; be it family, religion, political group, work force, etc.

In essence, the child grows up in a certain social group or setting. It is communicated to him/her that within the group are the opportunities and limitations that life offers them. To move outside the group brings emotional conflicts and confusion; depending upon the distance one removes oneself.

Conforming to the expectations seems to be the lesser of the two evils; because within the group, an 'outcast' is someone who drops below OR rises above the group's expectations.

Those that fall below become known as the 'black sheep' of the family. They often do not fit in anywhere. I tend to think that it takes more courage to do this than to conform. At least, they have chosen to follow their own path.

The ones that rise above are usually the ones that do not seem to be absorbing this aspect of the enculturation process either. When you become aware of these individuals, you realize that their reality is being shaped by something else. This 'something' else may be schooling (books), travel, television, a mentor, or a greater knowing from the depth of their being that speaks to them, guides them, and reassures then that their life has its own path. It gives them the freedom to soar.

# 9

## Daddy Comes Home

Summer – 1945

*Life was nicer than it had ever been.*

I often wondered why the Army took my dad. He was 35 years old and had five children to care for. He was one of the few who made it through D-Day. In all, he spent 16 months on the front lines. Because he had spent his life hunting for a living and was a 'sharpshooter,' during many months of his tour of duty he was sent out to scout for the enemy ahead of his troops. He was trained to spot squirrels in the trees, and he could quickly determine the nuances of color in a tree, on the ground, and at a distance; thus spotting enemy troops or a sniper and bringing him down before his patrol was in danger. He talked of long marches through the snow. He told of every one having frost bite on their faces, hands and feet. Many fell and had to be left behind. Keeping their feet dry, he told me was, in fact, a matter of staying alive.

He talked about his Uncle Ode, his dad's brother who had been dead for several years, of being with him during the war. One day, late in the afternoon, everything was quiet. Dad stood in the foxhole with his rifle resting on the top. Uncle Ode appeared in front of him. Using the palm of his hand, he knocked my dad flat in the foxhole just before a mortar round went off near his hole. He came again the night before dad's troops jumped off the Rhine River to move down into Paris. He stood at the foot of the bed and told my dad that he would be wounded the next day, but he would not be sent home.

Dad did, in fact, spend a few weeks in the hospital in Paris. Then he rejoined his outfit for a few weeks of patrolling the streets of Paris. He talked of his time in Paris and the other young men. None of them expected to return home. "If they had a nickel," he would say, "they spent it on booze and women." "They treated each day as their last."

He had begun with a North African campaign. He went from there to D-Day. Many battles and hardships followed until he was wounded and sent to Paris for recovery. And from there he went back north to the Ardennes for six weeks of battles. Later in the year of 1944 he fought in both France and Belgium and was later wounded in the Battle of the Bulge. In the Battle of the Bulge he received shrapnel to the right side of his face and in his right shoulder. They were unable to remove the shrapnel. He was sent home.

At five, I seemed to be seeing my dad from a new perspective. His jaw and his shoulder would start to quiver because the shrapnel was lying against nerves. Then his whole body would join in and eventually he would be shaking all over. I watched as he would collapse on the floor. In a few moments he would rise. As I observed during those years I was home with him and mom, I would wonder what horrors he was reliving each time his body gave way to the nerve attacks. It seemed like he was falling again in battle and facing death a thousand times. He shied away from people. But took his mustering-out money from the government and bought a pair of horses and equipment, and Old Betsy, our four-gallon-a-day milk cow. And he rented land to farm near Marked Tree, Arkansas.

Life was nicer than it had ever been for me. Our home was larger, our barn was larger. Our garden was large. Our pasture was large. Wow! Dad put everything he had into that land. And it provided well. Mom did too. My brother Roy was born. My sister Frances met her husband. She was 15. Mother had first married at age fourteen, so there was no problem with the marriage. But I missed her. Frances was the only one who gave me any care, and I felt alone.

There was much to be done on that farm, and everyone had many chores. We had a water pump between the house and the barn. Each day Jim and I pumped a trough of water for the horses and we also carried water to the house. Sometimes we filled #3 wash tubs for baths and filled the large iron kettles outside for the wash. Betsy, our cow, and the pigs were also watered. Jim had to toss hay to the bins for the cow and horses and I had to sit for long periods of time churning milk on the front porch for butter. I would carry Dad a quart jar of water to drink in the fields and sometimes I would stay and ride one of the horses home at the end of the day.

One day I was riding high on a wagon load of corn that Dad was taking to the barn. As we rolled into the yard, I heard someone call "Fay." But it was too late. Someone had been holding the clothes line up for the horses to get by and had to release it to open the gate. Dad had grabbed the line and ducked under it and let it fall in front of me, assuming that I would duck also. But I was having too much fun to notice. The clothes line caught me under the chin. I did a complete flip as I sailed off the wagon. Luckily, I landed on my bottom! But I was having the time of my life. Dad was working, Mom was cooking, and I had room and freedom to explore.

By October, all the crops and the garden were in, the pigs had been butchered and there was meat in the smokehouse. Row after row of canned fruit and vegetables lined the cellar. Sweet potatoes and Irish potatoes were there also. Jim and I had split wood and stacked it for the winter fires.

But to everything there is a season. Nancy, who had played all summer with her imaginary friend, Imogene, came in crying to say that her friend had died. She was three and had had Imogene to play with for some time. I missed her too, because she had always seemed to be there. But on a deeper level, I sensed that manufacturing a friend who loves you and cares about you was not working for her anymore. Her developing consciousness was telling her that she was only hiding from the truth; that she, in fact, actually had no one; the same as me. It seemed that to more than one of us, good things were coming to an end.

When summer came to a close we found ourselves pushed inward. Everyone was exhausted from the long spring and summer toil of planting and harvesting crops. They tried to busy themselves; although there was little to do inside the house.

The old life was beginning to come back as mother's temper flared. It took me a while to put the pieces together. With jumbled words and unfinished sentences things were going from bad to worse. Mother would explode and dad would defend. It only began making sense when Dad took Nancy on his knee one day and said to her quietly, "I am not your real dad". Neither of us was sure what that meant. Later I heard him say to my mother, "If we do, they will put him in jail for the rest of his life".

I only put it all together years later. But from information mother gave me later in life, I learned that when dad had left for his army boot camp, Grandpa and dad's youngest brother, who was 19 years old at the time, got drunk. They came by our house. Uncle Bill raped mother. Grandpa tried, but he had too much alcohol in him. The result was mother's pregnancy with Nancy. Mother was so hurt and angry at carrying the child of a rape. And to make matters worse, not even her husband would do something about it. Even Grandma took it lightly, saying things like, "All young men will sow their oats." "Men get drunk, and just do things they shouldn't." The fact that Dad would side with his mother and brother, against her, made Mother furious.

I had come to know when Mother was unhappy, every one was unhappy. And the families took sides.

The winter was cold with ice, snow, and freezing temperatures that made travel difficult at best and impossible for me as a frail six year old. Someone must have asked why the children in our family were not in school. Because, mom and dad went into town, on the wagon, and came back with shoes for me and Jim. I had wondered why she had drawn a picture of my foot on a piece of brown paper. I could not remember ever wearing shoes before. These shoes were bigger than my feet. But it was explained to me that there was extra room in the shoes for socks and for my feet to grow. There were also new clothes for Jim and a coat for me (I always wore his hand-me-down clothes). The coat was a reversible one, with red wool on one side, and a tan, woven, repellant fabric on the other side. It came to my ankles and I had to roll up the sleeves.

A few days later we were wading through the snow to go to school. I wasn't sure what school was, but was told I should like it and to do my best.

We started out at first light of day. The cold wind froze my hands and face. I slid and stumbled trying to walk in the deeply cut wagon ruts on the semi-graveled road. It was impossible for me to walk in the snow that came up to my knees on either side of the ruts. Jim walked on the other side of the road. Like always, he had to be as far from me as he could be. But he had been admonished by Dad to take care of me. That was probably the only thing that prevented him from leaving me behind and alone on the road. His legs were longer, and physically, he was stronger in forging through the snow and ice.

It was six miles between our house and the school. We made it to the school house a bit before noon. And when school let out at mid-afternoon, it was dark before we could arrive back home.

Both mom and dad had worried looks on their faces when we came through the door. Both of them began immediately to rub and massage our frozen feet, hands and faces. We were set next to the fire and all our wet clothing was removed. We were wrapped in quilts. And from the looks of things, this was an experiment that had gone bad. We did not go back to school that winter.

**Zalora Price**

I think that day became the deciding point for our family. Daddy said the family had to leave Arkansas so we could go to school. There were four other families, our relatives, who moved to Missouri at the same time. All that was left in Arkansas were Grandma and Grandpa in Marked Tree, and Uncle Bill and Aunt Jean in Lepanto. Our family had split. Those who were for looking the other way, and those who were facing the truth about the crime committed against my mother.

# 10

## Move to Missouri

1947 - Clarkton, Missouri

> *How long can a person go without validation, and still survive.*

Spring time, 1947, found us living in a wood frame house at the corner of two sandy roads, outside of Clarkton, Missouri. Dad had pocketed the money from the sale of our farm equipment and livestock. He had taken a house for 'day workers,' until he could find 'a little place of his own,' as he would say. The house was airy because of its poor construction. There were only the outside frame walls, with neither insulation nor inside finish. The floors were of rough pine with a lot of separation between the boards. Because the house sat on blocks as a foundation, I would have to say that we were very close to nature. The one thing I did love was the corrugated tin roof that seemed to sit loosely on the upright walls. I would lie at night and listen to the rain pinging on the roof. It seemed to break the silence of my life.

We supposedly moved to Missouri to get us enrolled in school. But even though the school bus passed our house everyday, we were not enrolled.

It was a difficult spring for everyone in our family. None of the siblings had had any childhood immunization shots. And

## Deprivation Trauma

once the diseases started, they moved from child to child every two weeks. It started with the mumps, which was very hard on all of us. It had the adults giving worried looks at each other. I was left very weak and remained immobile for another two weeks while my brother, Jim, fought his battle. Then come the measles; followed by the whooping cough.

When June came, my energy was truly spent. I sat in the sandy yard watching an occasional car go by. My fingers sifted the sand, but I rarely moved. I just couldn't seem to move or think. My body had been pushed to its limits. Mother must have known. She did not hesitate to slap me, but there were no beatings that spring.

Thank Goodness, chicken pox did not come until I started school.


Shortly after school was out that year, I experienced something that would cause me to question the reality I had been creating with my family.

It was a bright and sunny Sunday in July that some cousins came to see us. Brother Jim, leading the gang, decided to walk down the road to a railroad overpass. I trailed along. About half way there, we came upon an old house sitting on the left hand side of the road. Standing at an open window, beside the front door, was an older woman. She glared at us even before we reached the house. I knew right away that she did not like children, and did not want us there. I moved to the far right side of the road, as far as I could get. But, as we came closer, the ominous feeling I got made my feet feel like clay. I slowed. Then I stopped. And turned around and hurried home.

The others returned later and asked why I did not go with them. I told them it was because of the woman in the house. They laughed at me and all agreed that the house was only a rundown shack. It had been abandoned long ago. It was not only empty, but also uninhabitable.

They went on to play. I sat in the sand to wonder if I had really seen what I thought I saw. How had I known what the woman was thinking? And, was I indeed crazy, as they had said I was?

Have you ever felt that you were out in left field, on the opposite side of a coin, or on a different page, with those around you? How long can a person go without validation and still survive? These were the questions I began to consider. Do you keep putting yourself in a position to be questioned, or do you withdraw because you are the minority and cannot win? Who do you trust; yourself or someone else? My conclusion each time was that I had a different reality. And I would not give up who or what I was to be loved by them. I would not! I had to be me. Even if it was a secret me.

# 11

## Disaster

Summer - 1947

> *We were poor as poor can be, and could we survive?*

Since the weather was warm and the water down at the St. Francis River had warmed up, it was decided that our family and the family of my brother-in-law, who lived at Brosley, Missouri, would go swimming. We arrived at the river, excited about having hours of fun in the water. Some members of the other family were already in the water.

Daddy had fished in the river many times for catfish. He knew the water could be very deep in places. Standing on the bank, he saw my brother-in-law's brother in the water, with the water up to his neck. He immediately dove into the water. What he thought was six feet or more, was only about thirty inches. The person was sitting in the water, instead of standing or floating.

Dad's head hit the bottom with all the force of the dive. His body floated to the top, his face down. I heard screaming as they pulled him out of the water. The adults knew that he was badly injured.

Somehow, they got him into the back seat of a car. Knowing that his neck was probably broken, they packed bundles of sand

## Deprivation Trauma

around his neck so it would not move while they drove him to the Veterans Hospital in Poplar Bluff, Missouri.

X-rays showed not only a broken neck, but also several broken and slipped vertebra in his back. At one point in his neck, the vertebra had slipped sideways and was holding the spinal cord between two of them. "One slip," the doctor had said, "and the cord would be severed," and he would be paralyzed for life, "if he lives."

The hospital in Popular Bluff was not equipped to take care of him. So, they moved him again. This time he was in an ambulance, with Mother squatting beside him, holding the sand bags, to another hospital in Memphis, Tennessee.

The doctors in Memphis saw no way to operate on him, without killing him. They made the decision to drill two holes in his skull. And after putting tongs in his skull, they began to add weights daily. Four months later, when they reached sixteen pounds, the vertebra holding the spinal cord separated enough to allow the spinal cord to return to a position where the doctors could do more.

At that point, they took him to surgery. Using copper wires, they wired the vertebra in his neck and back together.

A year and a half passed before he could return home. During these months, Mother spent as much time with him as possible. Memphis was a long way from our home. Even thought the Veterans hospital provided for most of Dad's care, other related expenses took all our money, with little remaining to us for essential subsistence.

With all our money gone and Dad unable to work, we were 'doomed' to 'day work' to survive. 'Day work' meant that we worked, or were able to make some money, when someone needed something done. Since Jim and I were too young to hire out as day hands, that left only Mother to provide for the six of us. But, when the crops were ready to bring in, we could all help in the field. My tow sack filled with cotton only brought a few cents. But, I was doing my share.

We had been farmers in Arkansas, and we knew that the winter months would bring harsher weather further north in Missouri, with no work, no money, and little food. We were as poor as poor can be, and could we survive? That question remained to be answered.

# 12

## Time Again For School

Fall - 1947

> *They were laughing, and saying "Look at her. She has on a coat, but no shoes."*

Summer had been muggy. The Mississippi River Basin area flourished with mold and mosquitoes. This only added to the dismal conditions that already existed with the run down house, muddy roads, cistern water, and the mere essentials for existence.

The sheer exhaustion of the summer labor had taken its toll on everyone in the family. Each family member had their place and responsibilities. And the struggle for survival took precedence over personal attention.

Personal hygiene consisted of pumping a pan of cold water and the use of a harsh soap when the accumulation of dirt and dead skin cells became too itchy to tolerate.

My resistance to physical and mental blows caused me to be the last one to the table to see if there was anything left when the others were finished eating and out of the kitchen. Since it was my job to clean the dishes after meals, they knew I would show up at some time. Little, if anything, was ever left to eat. If Mother baked a pan of cornbread with the intent of it lasting for the next

## Deprivation Trauma

day's meal, and I took a bite of it, she would scream at me and beat on me.

My body was small for my age; just skin over bones. And my thin red hair looked ragged and unkept. My feet were crusty and scarred from exposure and going without shoes. I did not notice.

There was only an occasional day of work now. And fatigue permeated the environment. The day hands counted what little coins remained after their debts were paid at the general store, and worried about how they were going to be able to get through another winter. If they had enough money, they would buy a bag of salt, fifty pounds of pinto beans, rice, flour and lard. Coffee and an occasional slab of bacon came next. Rice was served for breakfast. And a little 'grease-gravy' made it more palatable day after day. The grease-gravy was made by adding a little bacon grease to brewed coffee, and then it was poured over the rice. A bowl of beans from the pot on the stove was served for dinner.

It was late fall when the crops were 'laid by' and there was little work left to be done in the fields. It was then decided that it was time for us to go to school. I would soon be seven years old. But, because I had never been in school, I was added to the first grade list.

The school was an old, square, brown brick building. It stood in the middle of a city block with a large, barren school yard in the center of Clarkton, Missouri. Grades 1-3 were downstairs. Grades 4-6 were upstairs.

The first frost arrived in early October. We awoke cold and with no wood for the stove. Our four room bungalow was framed with half inch thick pine boards and had no insulation. Mom always looked for one with tar paper covering the outside. But I would assume that out of necessity she had taken the one we were in. Air whipped up through the cracks in the wood floor and whistled around the window frames with their dirty panes. Our furnishings were meager. Nothing covered the windows to hold out the cold. A bed was the only piece of furniture in the bedroom. I rumbled through the piles of clothing scattered around the room. Finding a homemade hand-me-down dress, I pulled it on over my cotton long johns.

Someone called, "The bus is coming."

I ran to the front porch. My frail body shook with the onslaught of frost and cold air. Turning, I raced to the bedroom to find something with long sleeves to protect my small body.

"Hurry!" someone shouted from the other end of the house.

"I'm cold!" I shouted back.

Mother arrived and began to help me search through a pile of clothing in the corner. Digging underneath, she withdrew a hand-me-down coat that had been outgrown by someone in our extended family.

"Put this on," she said.

Putting my arms into the sleeves and wrapping the ladies short coat around me, I ran to reach the school bus just before the door was closed. All the while I was still trying to find my hands in the sleeves that reached down to my knees, and kicking the length that reached my ankles as I climbed the steps of the bus. The bus driver looked at me with a cold frown that said, "Don't ever plan on me waiting for you." I didn't. But I also knew how often he waited at a nice house down the road for a brother and sister who never ran and always looked like they had just been scrubbed and pressed.

He gave a strong jerk and accelerated the bus, as I gripped the back of the seats and made my way down the aisle looking for a place to sit. In each row sat students who shook their heads that said 'no,' I could not sit with them. Somewhere near the rear of the bus there were always seats. Only, the further back I sat the more nausea I had when I got to school. Many times I would dry heave because there was nothing in my stomach to throw up.

When school had started a group of first grade students

were put in the second grade classroom because the first grade teacher could not take all of us. I was in the group placed in Mrs. Shepherd's second grade class.

When I entered the second grade classroom, Mrs. Shepherd sneered at me, as usual, and turned her attention to the class. I took out a first grade reading book, but turned my attention to the second grade class being taught. I was lost in reverie when the bell rang, interrupting a wonderful story on historical events.

"Everyone outside for recess," came the instructions. I moved coyly down the hall to the front entrance. Caught up in the sweeping motion of everyone moving out of the building, I found myself flowing down the steps and on to the barren earth. My cold feet responded to the sharp rocks and shattered glass that was spread across the school yard. When things cleared, I moved back to the sidewalk, and then to the top step by the door. The sun was shining, but the sharp wind cut through my thin hair. Standing on the concrete steps was like standing on ice. Shivering, I wrapped the coat around me and pulled my hands inside the sleeves. I stood anxiously waiting for the bell to ring again.

In front of me, on the sidewalk, girls were playing jump rope. I shifted from foot to foot, resting one on top of the other for warmth. One of the girls said something to one of the other girls. Then another. And another. In seconds they were all looking at me. And they were pointing their fingers at me. And laughing! "Look at her." They were saying. "Look at her. She has on a coat but no shoes."

Recess became a horror. There were both physical and psychological attacks. Children I did not know would come by me, just to punch at me. Others 'made fun' of me in every conceivable way. Their talk, whispers, and giggles, told me I was an outcast, disliked, and unwanted, because I was poor.

The bell rang. I couldn't tell if the shrill, piercing ring was the school bell or the panic bell going off in my head. They were one and the same. Recess!!!

I waited for further instructions. None! That meant we did not have to go outside. But my mind did not have enough time to settle before I heard, "Go play." That meaning, "everyone out of the building."

"Play!!" "Play!!" My mind repeated.

Horror swept over me as my mind fought for control. My body wanted to remain in the seat with a safe distance between me and the others. My mind wanted to remain with the books, to know more about the people and places found there. My body shivered at the thought of the outside cold temperature.

Books. My haven. Their words told me of another world where people were comfortable, happy and adventurous. This world in the books was so different from my own.

I moved to go out the door, slowly behind the others.

Instead, I went past the outside door, deeper into the hallway as the others pushed past me. I cautiously observed things around me for a while. The other classrooms in that end of the building were quiet. They were out for recess also. Unconsciously, I had moved into streams of sunlight coming through the large overhead windows of the hallway. My body was constantly yearning for warmth and light. I had placed my hands into my coat pockets. My hand felt something in the pocket. The object came out partially entwined with a nose rag. It was a small piece of a mirror that had belonged to my mother. Just a small, broken piece. But big enough that I could see my nose, or my eye. My nose had large, brown freckles on it like the ones on my arms and hands. My eyes looked back with a kindness and of a color combination of teal and green. I contemplated the mirror and my reflection. I had seen mirrors, but could not remember having one in our house since living in Arkansas two years earlier.

I tilted the mirror to see my hair. The bright red hair lay like golden strands against my head and the strands seemed to dance in the light as I moved my head. I was Grandpa Johnson's favorite grandchild because of my red hair. He was proud of our ancestry. And I was the first child in America with the family trait since his father had left the British Isles after a bloody political battle. Those thoughts always came when I was feeling alone and different.

It seemed at that moment the ceiling above me lit with light, as if a light bulb had come on! When I looked up, the light moved. The mirror piece was reflecting sunlight. I played with the light; throwing it into all the dark corners, on the floor, ceiling and walls. I was so engrossed with the dancing light that I had not heard Mrs. Shepherd coming down the staircase. When the light hit her, it was too late. The look on her face told me of her disgust, and at the same time, her delight at 'crushing' my spirit. Without a word, she walked to me, put out her hand, and took the mirror. She then turned and walked into the classroom.

I stood confused. The light must be a bad thing. I would not play with light anymore.

When the bell rang to go home I approached her desk. "Can I have my Momma's mirror?' I ask shyly.

"The mirror was only a broken piece that no one would want so I threw it away," she replied.

Life? Mine seemed to be a series of broken pieces. The pieces left me in confusion, and sometimes despair. The more I thought about things, the more confused I often became. Most of the time nothing concerning the people around me made sense to me. I began to envision life as a jigsaw puzzle, and tried to put the pieces together. When my common sense did not work, I tried other approaches by looking at what I considered could be other people's logic.

I reasoned Mrs. Shepherd disliked my mother, and therefore threw away her mirror. No, Mrs. Shepherd did not know my mother. Mrs. Shepherd does not like me and wants to hurt me. No, I am always polite, well-mannered, and well-behaved in class. I always have my class work completed on time, and with 100's. Then, Mrs. Shepherd LIKES to be unkind. No, I could not see how anyone could like to be unkind.

But SOMETHING makes Mrs. Shepherd, my mother, and

the other children act the way they did. But what was it? The more bits and pieces I generated only provided more confusing options. All of which did not fit into either my family or the school situation. Many of my puzzle pieces were apparently missing. I was determined to keep watching and listening and reading for information.

My attempts at understanding my family and the world around me drew me into exploring my consciousness more objectively that year. The hours I spent alone was dedicated to understanding why I was different. I concluded that I did not mind being different because I was a better person than the ones who caused me pain and suffering. The way I thought, my opinions, my choices, always seemed to conflict with those around me. I wanted to be kind and have others treat me kindly. But it was not reciprocated. I wanted an education. My family was not interested in an education for me and Mrs. Shepherd did not want to teach me. When I wanted to share my ideas, nobody wanted to listen. I showed others respect. They treated me with disrespect. I seemed to have been born into the wrong family. Was I also in the wrong universe?

# 13

## I Could Hold My own

Fall - 1948

> *I knew that when it came to using my mind, I could hold my own with anyone. I knew I had found a means of survival.*

If the first grade brought pain, the second grade brought gain. A gain in respect. While it had not been her intention, Mrs. Shepherd's lack of attention to her small flock of first graders had allowed for the total absorption of the second grade material by my alert mind.

I had sat quietly, as required of me. The time alone in the classroom felt like a blessing to me. No one was hitting me. No one was yelling at me. The space around my desk was like an island away from the world. I quietly sat, enjoying the stories in the reading books, history stories, practicing the math facts, and spelling along with the spelling bees. I watched as, over and over, the spelling words and math facts were written on the blackboard. I listened as the others read aloud and responded to social studies questions. My mind absorbed it all, recording every detail, bringing it into the vivid, exciting world of my imagination. My mind played it out, making it a part of me. Mrs. Shepherd's tall stoic figure, with her cold eyes and stern face became lost in the bland and dark classroom, while my heart and mind found a wonderful place of its own. It was not my class. But I learned the second grade material, just the same.

Now the school year began, again, in the room next door to Mrs. Shepherd's classroom.

When I opened the door, my eyes blinked. The morning sun was pouring through the windows. The walls were covered with color. There were pictures of animals, letters, and everything imaginable! And there stood Mrs. Overall; four foot, eight inches, and every part of her was round. But the brightest and most marvelous part of her was her face, with her happy, twinkling eyes.

I stood just inside the door trying to take it all in. I was still without words as Mrs. Overall greeted me and showed me to a seat in front of the room near her desk. It was going to be a good year. I just knew it!

And I found out soon enough on the first Friday. Friday was the day for Spelling Bees, math facts on the board, and show and tell. The winners of the spelling bee and math facts remained at the black board until defeated. The problem arose when Johnny and I could not be defeated and could not defeat each other. And being so equally matched, we became team leaders in any event. In the end, when all the others were down, and only the two of us were left, it would become a draw. So, neither team ever lost.

It was a huge ego boost for me, to go from 'outcast' to 'leader.' The students, who had been cruel to me, now screamed my name, begging me to put them on my team. Even though I wore my clothes straight off the clothes line, they were clean and I had also learned the importance of keeping my face and hands clean, and to comb my hair before going to school.

Just starting the second grade of school I was beginning to feel good about myself and was building some self-esteem, and confidence that I had other skills for survival. It was a wonderful new feeling for me since my hope had been fading.

I knew now that I could be an important person. I also knew that when it came to using my mind that I could hold my own with anyone. I knew I had found a means for survival in the outside world! And if it came to the point where I thought I might not survive at home I was not afraid to go out into the world.

# 14

## A Step Forward, A Step Back

1949

> *A child, who grows into adulthood without the benefit of customs, standards, celebrations, rules, regulations, expectations, or even anticipation, finds confusion when attempting to establish norms for their own family."*

After my first full year of school in the second grade, it all ended. All the pride and excitement! I had had a position and none of my peers could top me. My brain was like a weapon I could use to defend myself and bring me respect and consideration. Mrs. Overall was nurturing and kind. Oh! How I hated to leave school for the summer.

During the late summer, Dad was finally allowed to return home from the hospital. He came home wrapped in a cast from the top of his head to his hips. He had been instructed to wear it for several weeks.

During his year and a half in the hospital, things had gone from bad to worse for our family. We had no money left. The day jobs barely put beans on the table. We moved three times during

## Deprivation Trauma

my third grade year. And we only attended a few days of school at each location. There was no money for clothing, shoes, or lunch money. Mom was doing the best she could, working at anything she could. Jim and I worked at anything we could. That included picking cotton until the last boll was gone.

Then the winter months immobilized us, because of the lack of wood or coal for our stove, and any degree of proper clothing to protect us from the elements. The lack of activity was probably good, since our bodies lacked nourishment.

Cold! Hunger! No school! I was born for more than this! I knew it! My mind screamed! But when, where, how?

Winter suffered on. I spent days upon days trying to stay away from the others in the house. I still had no respect at home. Jim still hurt me. Mother still slapped me around when I was within reach. No one talked to me. They talked 'around' me, as if I was not there. It was okay with me by this time, because I had come to know that I was not a part of the family. And I spent a great deal of time alone, still wondering why I was there and when I could leave.

During this year we had moved for the third time. I don't remember the reason for the move. But I vividly remember the house and an event following the move.

This time, the four room bungalow sat out in the middle of a cotton field that had been harvested. The ridges of cotton rows extended for miles around us. It would have been muddy around the shack, but the ground was frozen and ice crunched under our feet when we were outside. Sheets of ice filled the furrows where there had been repeated raining and freezing. Coal smoke rose up from the chimney and had deposited a layer of coal dust on the asbestos roof leaving it dark and streaked. More would swirl through the air and fall upon us, leaving black smudges on our clothing. The drafts of wind around the house made the soot look like black snow as it pulled the soot in mass away from the house.

There came a day I will always remember. I think I remember the day so vividly because of the sunshine. Sunlight, or lack thereof, always played a significant role in my well being. I think my body longed so much for warmth that my spirit immediately lifted at the first hint of sunshine.

On this particularly cold winter day the sun was shining. The sky had cleared to a clear, light blue, with nothing in the sky but the blue and the golden rays of sunlight. I felt wonderful! My mind seemed to 'wake-up' from its winter sleep.

Company came. Aunt Dot, Uncle Jay, and children. There were five children in our family and five children in their family. Each of us had a near twin in age, in the other family. In addition, we were double first cousins. (Brother and sister had married brother and sister.)

All of us (children) were in the yard when an eleven or twelve year old said something about it being Christmas. "Is this Christmas Day?" I asked.

"Mother said not to tell anyone," came the reply. 'Anyone' meant the six younger children.

I ran to the house.

"I want to put up a tree," I announced.

"We don't have a tree to put up." Mother snarled, trying to ignore me.

"I know. I'll find one," I said.

"There's nothing to decorate it," She stated.

"We'll make some decorations," I countered.

The others had followed me inside. "Yeah. Let's put up a Christmas tree."

Realizing the story was out, and not wanting to be harassed anymore by the kids, a nod for approval was given for the venture.

Outside, my eyes looked up and down the cotton rows. Clearly, nothing in sight looked like a Christmas tree. But not being easily swayed, my eyes landed on a cotton stalk. It had symmetrical limbs. Why not? Looking further, I spotted one with unopened boles and burrs with some stringing locks of cotton. Pulling fiercely on it would not release it from the ground, until we had all pulled on it.

Carrying our 'tree' inside, we set it up in a galvanized 'coal bucket' and packed chunks of coal around it. Now we had our tree. But it had to be decorated. We went through the house and found several empty cigarette packages. Removing the foil paper from inside the packs, we wrapped them around our fingers and twisted them at the top. We ended up with several silver bells. We tied white sewing thread around the twist and looped them over the branches of the stalk. Various other colorful things were found, and placed on or near the 'tree'. Standing back, we admired our work. And we felt happy knowing it was a holiday.

The adults continued their conversation as if the 'tree' was not there. Maybe denial was easier for them.

A child, who grows into adulthood without the benefit of customs, standards, celebrations, rules, regulations, expectations, or even anticipation, finds confusion when attempting to establish norms for their own family. As an adult, I found planning something as simple as a birthday party or a family Christmas dinner bewildering to me since I had no example to follow.

In a family where there are no holidays, no fun activities, no gifts, no vacations, nor fairy tales, a child, by social standards, may appear retarded or possibly depressed. Fear and a lack of response, from a child or adult, can present itself as dullness and can be misleading. When, in fact, the child may not have known joy or know how to create it.

The average child, with reasonable care and nurturing, grows up learning to be spontaneous, being interested in things, experiencing the thrill of knowing about things, and pursuing their interest. Through parental nurturing, expectations are created for behavioral norms. Having the right and ability to choose and make choices would be considered normal development. But, when the toils of life repress or take away those things which allow for normal social interactions, the person becomes reserved and confused about social expectations.

Social skills are an important factor in our society. Most of us do not have a choice in deciding if we will work alone or with others. Even if we work alone most of the time, our success may depend upon our success in dealing with others in the business community. And it doesn't end there. We have extended families and community interests. There are norms set up for behavior, verbal usage, and expectations. They are normally learned from our family of origin, in the home. Otherwise, they must be learned 'as you go' through trial and error, while the person tries to stay in the good graces of those around him/her.

Simple things for some may become major problems for a person who has not had the family experiences to fall back on. A decision on the proper attire (formal, dressy, sporty) for an occasion, food/table etiquette, what kind of gift and cost for a gift, and topics of conversation acceptable for certain occasions are rooted in the family. Housekeeping (and home maintenance) and décor, budgeting financial assets, and a personal style, all have roots in the family. While things can be learned in adulthood through observation, reading, and questioning, the deprivation experienced in childhood has a life-long effect as the adult struggles to learn and adjust to social standards and expectations.

For most families there is orderliness about life. There is a work schedule, a time for worship, chore time, meal time, and a time for relaxation. Children thrive on structure. They like a framework in which to function. This is because they do not have the experience to make a judgment call in many situations. They also want to please and would prefer to be told in simple terms the expectations of the parents/guardians. Without expectations, the child grows into adulthood unable to set priorities, unable to plan, and does not have the mind set of being goal-orientated. They may lack the organization in their personal lives and in the workforce to succeed in either.

Only through intense desire can they find the strength to struggle forward, through failed attempts, to keep pace with the demands of our modern society. They may sit on an assembly line and do a single chore daily for their livelihood without having to prioritize their day. But when they pick up their paycheck on Friday, is the money spent at the local tavern, the dress shop, on the car, or a lottery ticket before the electric bill is paid or money put aside for school lunches for the children. If never taught to exercise control and to create order and structure in youth, then the person learns these by fear, embarrassment, and sometimes physical and mental suffering in adulthood. Creating joy and beauty may only come later when they can manage life in general.

# 15

## Those Pesky Mosquitoes

1949 - Bell City Schools

*"She has a fever,"* I heard someone say.

Somehow we missed summer school. Either we were not on a school bus route, or we had not attended enough school for the past two years that the idea just didn't occur to my parents to locate the nearest school, or to make an effort.

Whatever the reason, late September found us at still another location and riding the school bus to the Bell City Schools. I suppose by age only, I was placed in the fourth grade class.

In 1949, the mosquitoes had become very bad in the Mississippi Basin. From unclean water, there were also several outbreaks of typhoid fever. It was announced one day that nurses were at the school to give everyone a 'shot' to prevent a typhoid fever epidemic.

I stood in line to see what 'getting a shot' was about. When I saw the long needles, I decided to not look when it came my turn.

The shot itself, hurt very badly in my thin arm. But I was not one to complain. As I walked away, my head felt dizzy. Someone caught me by the arm and sat me in a chair. I heard a nurse say,

"She looks pale." I don't know how long I sat there. I think my eyes were closed, because I do not know what was happening during that time.

Then I felt a hand lifting my wrist. "She has a fever," I heard someone say. The attenuated virus I had been given as an antigen seemed to accelerate the malaria from the mosquito's bites or the typhoid virus already in my body. Another shot was put into the other arm. I can only assume that it was an antibody. I was taken home to spend a couple of weeks wrapped in heavy quilts while running a high temperature.

I was back in school for a while before we moved again.

Summer: Bell City area (earlier that year)

It wasn't surprising that after ten years of isolation from most of my family and peers that I did not question the coming and going of a tall, young man who was a friend of my parents and who lived not far from us. When Mother told me to shut and lock the bedroom door, I simply did as I was told, assuming that they wanted privacy. It was not my place to question their behavior. I went about taking care of my responsibilities as usual.

I did not question his coming to the house when Dad was not there. And I did not question his coming when both Mom and Dad were not home. It was something that simple did not concern me. I had no say in family affairs. I had been beaten up enough that I was conditioned to not respond to anything that did not include me.

Neither did I question when he took Nancy's hand and said, "We are going into the corn field to play. I don't want the rest of you coming into the field."

Our house sat out on a lonely, back country road. Corn fields surrounded the house. The corn stood six feet tall. Because of the lack of yard, and because of the heat of the summer sun, the children often sat within the shade of the cornstalks. And, sometimes too, they played tag and hide and go seek there.

I looked at Nancy. She seemed comfortable with the idea of playing in the corn field with him. I nodded and went about my chores.

This was her second known series of sexual assaults. Unfortunately, I did not understand enough about what was happening to help her. As I look back, I remember her as a loving child who gave and sought attention. Being a sexual predator as he was, Nancy became easy prey. I, on the other hand, had come to demand that others stay away from me because my lack of trust issues had already developed.

Since becoming adults, Nancy and I remember his height, approximate age, his red plaid flannel shirt, and his beard. We cannot recall his name.

# 16

## Petty's Place

January - 1950

> *"Some things in the world, we can never explain," he said. It was like something profound that he was trying to teach me.*

Mother was pregnant again. But this time, she was not doing well. She had never had prenatal care but had done okay up until Roy, her sixth child. After Roy, she had two miscarriages. The last of which claimed the lives of twin girls who were born two months too early. Fortunately, for this pregnancy we were close enough to town for her to see a doctor and get a check-up. Unfortunately, the results of the check-up were not good. She had cancer of the uterus. She chose to wait until my sister was born in March to have surgery.

Winter - 1950

Winter had come with a beauty rarely seen in southern Missouri. The cold took on a frosty air. The morning broke with the glistening and tinkling of a winter fairyland. The ice clung to the tiniest branches; and icicles, long and short, reflected every ray of the warm, golden sun. The gentlest of breezes rocked and nudged the frozen blades of grass in the fields and on the hillsides.

Midday found the frost lifted and drops of sparkling diamonds of water dripping from the trees.

The days were short and the skies were mostly grey. Within a few hours, everything was refrozen again from the lack of sunlight. The cold temperatures at night would refreeze the ice for the coming morning for another beautiful day of fairyland.

Sheer determination came in the mornings just to leave the heavy quilts and touch our feet to the cold, wooden floors, and to dislodge the water that was frozen in the water bucket and wash pan.

Dad would lay a log on the ashes in the old wood stove. Minutes later a roaring fire would have the iron stove red hot, warming the surrounding area.

Children with squinting eyes, bare feet, and tousled hair, would join in the warmth. Each would find a place on the floor. They would first face the stove, then turn to warm their backs as they pulled on socks and shoes.

A pan of rice and a pan of biscuits was what it took to start the day. Water would be boiling in the kettle on the wood stove.

Later, the morning activities would be off and running. Shoes would be tied and coats buttoned. It was three miles, by road, to the school house. A trail across the pastures cut a little distance to the school, and was certainly the most scenic route. I had to climb over the bailing wire fence and under the barbed wire to get into the pasture. Walking sure-footedly over the ice and snow, I would follow the fence rows to assure my safety. Gullies crafted from erosion by the spring rains and now covered with snow were a short cut well missed. Cows sometimes fell into them and were later found dead.

I had started school, so briefly, in the fifth grade at Gideon, Missouri. But another move took us from town to the country, away from the competitive classroom I loved…to a one room school house with classes from first to eighth grade.

We now lived below Wilson Hill. It was, literally, a hill with our house near the bottom on the hillside. Our drive was a long way up to the main road. So we often took a short cut which was straight up, taking us through the cemetery lying just below the road.

The markers in the cemetery were old, and the small area lay nestled beneath the beautiful oaks of the Ozarks. It was a cool, shady place in the summertime. In the freezing winter months, the bare limbs were frozen with ice and glistened in the morning sun looking like a fairy land of intricate designs. It was a place for dreams and wonder. I would sit on a stone surrounded by the beauty. My mind would fill with the imagination of a lonely, whimsical, child.

Wilson Hill was a property that was part of a ridge of land rising out of a valley that reaches down to the Mississippi River in southeastern Missouri. Mother told us stories about the great earthquake that took many lives. She said that when the water started to raise from the river all the people started to run for the ridge. Many could hardly make it and literally crawled up the ridge on their hand and knees trying to outrun the flood waters. So the ridge was later called Crawlers Ridge.

Petty's land was near Wilson Hill. His son Roy Petty, and my brother Jim, became best friends. Roy had a small snow sled. He also had some coon hounds. I don't know whose idea it was but before long they had the sled stacked with girls. I would watch as they raced off to school with them shouting and laughing. I wanted so much to be a part of it. I would watch them from a distance. Then I would climb over the bailing wire, under the barbed wire and start out for school in my own direction.

The school house sat in an open stretch of land along the dirt road that wound through the country side. It was surrounded by farms of various sizes. The exterior was weathered grey wood.

## Zalora Price

On first approach the building looked to be one large room with an entry foyer in the front. The chimney rose from the roof in the back. I think it was all the windows along each side of the structure that said, "School House." There were no signs, banners, or mailbox.

When I opened the door I found there was a small kitchen on the left as I came in the front door. Coats and boots were placed on the opposite wall. Beyond that was the larger classroom with four rows of seats on the left and right sides of the room, and a large aisle down the middle. At the end of this aisle sat a large round pot belly wood stove. A teacher's desk with a blackboard behind it was on the right back corner across from the stove. Low double hung windows lined each side of the room for ventilation during the summer and transferred the cold air into the room in the winter months.

It was the teacher's job to arrive early to start a fire to warm the room before the children arrived. But it was usually the bigger boys who helped start the fire as we were arriving. We would sit huddled at our desks with our coats, hats, and gloves on to keep us warm. When it came time for attention to a particular grade, the students of that grade would move to the front of the room and sit on a bench seat next to her desk. She would speak quietly her instructions to those on the bench.

There were no fifth graders. I sat in a row with two fourth grade girls. I had been given two books. I had a social studies book and an English book. These were the only fifth grade books the school had. Lucky for me, I shared the fourth grade math book with the two fourth grade girls. Since I had only been in school a few weeks in the third and fourth grades, I was now able to catch up on the learning of fractions, which I had missed.

I was surprised when one of the girls handed me a piece of biscuit on the first day I was at the school house. I laid it up by my inkwell. "You can eat it," she said. I looked around. I suppose I was waiting for the teacher to yell at everyone to get quiet so class could begin. There was a kind of hum in the room, with groups of two to three students each talking in soft voices. What I came to realize was that the loosely organized students, who were allowed to drink water, chew gum, and eat, were also busy teaching each other.

There were very few requests to use the toilet. It was a good distance behind the school house. Going out in the cold was one thing, pulling down our pants and sitting on the wooden seat was another. The cold wind would whip through the one inch cracks in the wood frame walls, and up from the open back, blasting us on our bottoms. It took a great deal of concentration just to relax enough to tinkle down the hole.

Lunch was another surprise. The cook came from the kitchen and announced that lunch was ready. I stayed in my seat as I had always done, because I had never had money for lunch. I would sit in the classroom and read, or stand on the playground when I had to. But the two fourth grade girls were saying, "Come, everybody eats." I joined the line and took a plate of pinto beans, fried potatoes, and a piece of cornbread. It tasted good, and felt warm in my tummy. I was to learn, later, that the food in the kitchen was all donated by the parents of the students and the cook herself was a volunteer. We had very little to offer that first winter. But when Mother's garden started coming in, in the spring and peaches were available, we canned quart jars of green beans, whole tomatoes, new potatoes, butter beans, corn, carrots, cabbage, spinach, and peaches. We carried boxes of filled quart jars to the school house. We did not have money to donate, but one of the canned food items tasted good when added to our bean plate. The dried beans were our staple food item.

We had become share croppers with our move to Wilson Hill. That was a step up from being day workers. This meant our family took on the responsibility of planting, maintaining, and harvesting thirty acres of cotton. This was the customary amount for a family to handle. In this case, Mr. Petty supplied the horse and plow. We supplied the hoes, cotton sacks, gloves, etc. and worked the land. We lived on credit at the country store for six months while we were working the land and until the crops were harvested and sold. The owner of the land took out the cost of the seeds and half of the earnings. With the other half we paid our bill at the country store and paid back the 'draw' we received from the land owner. The general scenario was that there was little or nothing left. But we still had to make it from September until January when we could expect a 'draw' for food until 'day work' became available in March to May. It was what we called a 'hand to mouth' existence. We never had anything more than just enough to eat to keep us alive.

Katie, my baby sister was born in March. Mom spent weeks in the hospital after the surgery, and in bed at home.

I had also turned ten years old in March. Nancy turned six in April. She was able to spend a little time at school in the late spring. The lack of food and proper clothing had made it impossible for her to make it to school in the coldest weather. With Mother's illness, it had become my job to take over the household tasks and to care for the three little ones.

As such, it was my job to walk Nancy to school. I would try to encourage her along, but she would stop and cry. We would get to school late and get home late. When the sun goes down in the Ozark Mountains, it turns cold quickly. When we were caught on the road or trying to cut across pastures, the cold and the darkness made it even more difficult. She would also hurt herself trying to climb over the fences she selected which were too high for her, or get caught in the barbed wire. She would fall into gullies in the pasture because she would not follow the path I had laid out for her. I think at times she did it on purpose. Nancy knew that if she was hurt that it was an excuse for another beating for me. She was learning the 'family way' very quickly. If Mom beat on me enough, it kept Nancy safe.

That spring, I did manage to carry home a few of the reading (library) books from school. I loved the Bobsy Twins, and Freckles. When everyone went to bed, I would bring the oil lamp and sit it on the floor close to the stove, and read until the last of the fire from the stove was gone.

With Mother's illness in the spring, Dad would cook the rice for breakfast. Then he would be off to the fields. I would feed Nancy and Roy, and do the dishes. Mid-mornings I always loved the walks to the field to take drinking water to Dad.

One morning Dad had just finished the water I had taken him, when we heard a 'whof-whof' sound coming from the sky. In seconds, what looked like a grey, three inches deep by eight inch wide, by twelve foot long plank of wood (?) came into sight. It came at an angle and hit the earth about ten rows over from us. We broke into a run towards the site. We stopped as abruptly as we had burst into our run. We both stood staring down at the exact spot where the board had hit. Not a grain of dirt was disturbed! We looked at the spot, at each other, and back at the landing site. "Where is it?" I ask.

"Some things in the world we can never explain," he said.

It was like something profound that he was trying to teach me. We walked back to the plow.

"Sis" he said, "You think you can have some dinner cooked when I get home?"

"Sure." I said.

The cultivating and planting always started the first of February. And any good farmer had his crops 'laid by' by May 1st. Daddy's crops were done by the Almanac and always on time.

Our being in and out of school may seem a little confusing by today's standards. But we were an agricultural community and everyone's lives revolved around their crops. The school let out for the planting. There was a summer school. Then, the children were let out for the harvesting of the crops in September and October. Then everyone was back in school for the four winter months of November to February.

When I got back to the house I started picking the rocks and dirt clods out of the beans and washing them through several pans of water, which Mother had taught me to do. Usually, we would clean them and soak them overnight before cooking them. So I put them on the stove immediately knowing it would take much longer for them to cook without soaking them. I had been peeling potatoes for years and could wield a kitchen knife as well as any woman. Also, my Daddy was a biscuit man. When supplies were available, he loved his biscuits. When eaten with a hunk of butter, he would smack his lips and hum with delight. But I had never made biscuits!

Helping in the kitchen all those years had taught me the ingredients and about how much to use. So I got out the bowl and the breadboard. I mixed the dry ingredients with the water and the lard. After I had worked it with my hands to a smooth consistency, I sifted flour on to the board. The table stood at my chest. I had to raise my elbows to reach and knead the dough. In doing so, I had managed to get the flour across the front of my clothing. Mother came into the kitchen at that time. She took one look at what I was doing, and with a very stern face said to me, "Fay…a good cook is a clean cook," and left the room. I hastily dusted myself off and continued to roll out the dough. I cut it with the round tin biscuit cutter. I put melted bacon grease in the large iron skillet. Then I dropped the biscuits in the grease and turned them over, before placing them side by side in the skillet. And, as Mom would say, "I popped them in the oven."

When Dad got home, I set the table. The plates were spaced around the table, and the spoon and fork jars were put in the middle. The beans were a little firm. But Dad said they were alright, and would be perfect when warmed over for dinner tomorrow. He had that knack of making the most of any situation. I checked the biscuits and they looked a nice golden brown.

When I turned the skillet and dumped the biscuits on to a plate, they did not look right. They were flat and hard. I had forgotten the baking powder, which would have made them rise. Dad ate them just the same. Mom was quiet. Jim yelled at me, asking if there was anything I could do right.

I cooked, cleaned, did laundry by hand, and cared for Nancy and Roy. When the summer garden came along, I worked there also, tying the pole beans, staking the tomatoes, and hoeing and weeding the vegetables. I fed the chickens and brought in what few eggs they laid.

By August, Mother was feeling better. We cut corn from the cob, stringed and snapped green beans, dug and cleaned new potatoes, shelled butterbeans and black eyed peas, washed, cleaned and removed insects from spinach, scraped and chopped carrots, and parboiled and skinned tomatoes and peaches. Mother's canning pots stayed on the stove for many days. She would lift one set of jars from the pot and put another batch in. Then at night we would lie in bed and listen as the jars cooled and the lids would 'pop,' sealing the lids. We placed the jars on the shelves with the blackberries we had canned in the spring. Nothing took away the winter doldrums better than one of Mom's peach or berry pies.

There must have been a sense of community among the farm people. Mother loved to cook and had volunteered to cook at the school kitchen. And through some contacts in the area, she got word of a 'box-supper' to be held at the school. Now, a box-supper is an old-fashion way of bringing the community together for a social, and a cause. The cause in this case was for the school's needs. All the women were to bring a boxed supper which would be auctioned off to the men. The man or boy buying the box at auction would then share the meal with the girl or woman who had brought the box. Dad did not have the money to bid on Mom's meal. So, he stayed home and Mom brought me to the school with a box.

Box suppers were nothing new to Mom and Dad. Dad had eaten many a dry sandwich for a box at box suppers. Mom put into my box the bologna sandwiches with home made pickles, and raw carrot sticks. She cut two round holes in the box lid. Before closing it, she pushed the necks of two Coca Cola bottles through the lid. The box was tied with string and we left for the auction.

The summer night was hot with all the people crowded into the classroom. There was hardly room to breathe. And our throats were dry. When the auction started, all the eyes were going back and forth between the box in the auctioneer's hand and my box sitting there with the two coke bottles sticking out of the top.

Finally, the auctioneer picked up my box. Every male there seemed to get in on the action. It brought $1.25; the most any box sold for that evening. And there were some mighty handsome boxes to choose from. Some were wrapped in fancy colored paper, and with ribbons and flowers. The decorations were unlimited, and some were the size to feed a mule. But none of them had anything to drink!

A young man, probably in his early twenties, bought mine. He had probably been saving for months, and was hoping to get to eat with someone more his age. Maybe find him a 'beau.' But we both got a lot of attention as we drank our cokes. And Mom got lots of attention because it was her idea.

All in all, the two nickel cokes were a great sacrifice by Mom and Dad for the occasion. In our circumstances, it was very difficult to have self-esteem or a sense of pride. That evening, our family was able to 'hold its own' within the community. That was my first time for me to feel a sense of community. I wasn't personally involved, but I knew what Mom and Dad were feeling. And it felt good. There was a kind of belonging, acceptance, and goodwill.

Crops were 'laid by.' Then summer school began. Dad would help with the little ones. The walks to school were tiring, but nice. I appreciated everything about nature; the feel of warm soil between my toes, the sun on my face, the wind blowing through the trees and the flutter of their leaves. I enjoyed the rippling on the surface of the water in the tanks in the fields, birds and 'possums on the road, and inhaling the expanse of the world around me. The freedom of being alone in a beautiful landscape, the simplicity of walking alone on the tracks of a one lane dirt road to the little frame school house, that I loved so much, made me feel so light that I became fearful that I might blow away.

When I got to the school house one day, I found horses tied to the trees in the yard. Those who had horses had ridden them to school. Also, all the windows were opened wide to allow the breeze to flow through the classroom.

There were also times that summer when it was very hot in the classroom, and we would go outside and sit under one of the trees to study. There was a soft grass on the ground this time of year, and I loved the smell of new grass and fresh wild garlic.

But we only got to go back to school for a few days of the six weeks of summer school. This was because of an incident with Nancy and the teacher.

What I had first viewed as self-discipline in the kids at school soon became apparent to me that it was not by choice. Mrs. Chandler, the teacher, was a rather large woman. She would have looked like a man in her black suit, had it not been for her long skirt and her black hair pulled back in a bun. Her whole countenance was cold and her face fixed in a scowl. And behind her desk hung a two foot long, broad paddle with rows of round holes bored through it. Even the older, stronger boys, who questioned her resolve to use the board, never challenged the point again.

My sister Nancy was a willful child. She had been admonished to remain in her seat and work quietly. While it was not known at the time, Nancy was born a genius. The work given to her was completed far ahead of the others, and she actually needed other things to do. This was not the teacher's concern at the time. Her word was law. When she said "Sit," she meant, "Sit." When Nancy squirmed in her seat again, Mrs. Chandler took her board off the wall and walked to Nancy's desk. She reached for Nancy's hand and slammed the board across the palm. Nancy screamed and cried so that I had to lead her from the classroom and take her home. By the time we arrived home, large blisters ran across her entire palm. Mother was so angry that Dad had to talk her out of going to the school and attacking the teacher. Nancy did not go back to school. Soon, Jim and I were pulled out of school also.

Dad's cotton crop got us out of our winter debt from the previous year. But with nothing left over we were "living hand to mouth" as they would say, and we had no savings for getting us through the coming winter. There was some illness in the Petty family and they could not give us the 'draw' money we needed to get us through the winter.

It was moving time again!

# 17

## Lessons on Charity

Spring - 1951

> *I tasted it slowly, savoring the new flavor and the excitement of tasting candy.*

Spring found us in the Bell City, Missouri school district. Dad had found us another shack of a house that was isolated and surrounded by open fields and he was doing 'day work'. I took every opportunity to be on the school bus. Jim sometimes did and sometimes did not. He was getting old enough to keep up with the other day workers. His salary meant extra food on the table. Some landlords would allow him to work. Some would not.

Sixth grade in Bell City School was very difficult. There were cliques of boys and girls who spent a lot of the free time together. I heard talk about sex that I had never heard before. "See that one." one boy said. "I gave her six inches this weekend." And the girls in the group giggled. I also found out that many of the kids got to keep the money they made in the fields. They came to school dressed in new clothes and spent lots of money on snacks and drinks at the store across the street at lunch time. I had never had anything new to wear since the coat bought for me in the first grade. I received Jim's jeans and shirts when he outgrew them. He always got the new clothing. The girls in my class also wore pretty dresses and a few of them even wore lipstick. I wasn't comfortable in the situation. I stood on the school yard and watched.

"Hey you," one of the girls in my class was calling, and looking at me. I came closer to her. She thrust some money at me.

"Go over to the store and get me a mint patty. You can get yourself one also." I had already been thinking about the little store that everybody ran to when the noon bell rang. But I had no reason to go there. Now, I had some money in my hand and could go there and buy something. I had never actually bought anything before at a store. I wanted to do this.

I walked over to the little store at the edge of the school yard, and ask for two mint patties. Two were handed to me with change. I counted the change. I suppose I was lucky that he did not ask, "Which one?" I wasn't sure of what I was buying. I returned her change and her mint patty.

I walked away and opened my own mint patty. I took a small bite and realized that I had never tasted anything like it. The chocolate on the outside was almost bitter, but nice. The white mint inside was sweet, but strong. I tasted it slowly, taking very tiny bites. I savored the new flavor and the excitement of eating candy. "Candy." I had read the word in books.

The bell rang. I rewrapped the remaining half of the small round circle.

When the afternoon recess bell rang, I ran to the school yard and unwrapped the remaining half of the patty. I took tiny bites and let the mint and chocolate dissolve on my tongue. I wanted it to last as long as possible. I was so absorbed that I did not see the same girl walking by with her friends. "Are you still mincing around with that same piece of candy?" she asks. The other girls giggled.

I went for more candy and drinks. After a while, the newness wore off, and combined with their attitude toward me, I decided that I had had enough of being a 'runner' for my classmates.

After the harvest, I returned to school with a terrible cold. My nose was running so badly that I had to wipe it every few minutes. Before I left home, I looked everywhere around the house for something to use to wipe and blow my nose. The only thing I could find was a long one inch wide strip of fabric on Mom's sewing machine. It was a remnant left over from something she had sewn. I stuffed it into my pocket. I had noticed other kids using cloth handkerchiefs and even paper tissues. I tried to pull the long piece of fabric from my pocket as inconspicuously as possible when I needed it. The girl, who sat across from and behind me, kept watching me pull the fabric from my pocket. When she caught my glance, her expression changed from pity to kindness. I knew she was trying not to hurt my feelings by being rude. Others looked at me with sneers and disgust. That one look of kindness carried me through the few weeks that I remained in that school. I never knew her name because my attendance was very irregular.

# 18

## Turning Point

Fall - 1952

> *Mother stepped back as if she had been hit. She knew by the set jaw and the fire in my eyes, that the relationship between the two of us would never be the same.*

The summer passed quickly. Crops were harvested. And they were harvested much more quickly this year with the help of the new mechanical cotton pickers that were showing up around the country. My brother-in-law even got a job driving one for five dollars a day. But this only meant that day work was getting more scarce than usual.

Dad, Mom and Jim left early to look for work, or wherever their lives were taking them. Mother also took Katie because she was still on the breast. With Fran married, and Mother's illness, I had become the designated cook, housekeeper and babysitter.

Observing what they left behind from their breakfast I divided the small amount of rice left in the pan between Nancy and Roy. I knew that if either of them left a bite I would eat it later while I did the dishes. I had to stand to eat until I was ten years old. Now for the past two years there was not even a place for me at the table. When there was something left for me to eat I would just eat it on the go.

I got them dressed and seated at the table. While they were eating I went to the back yard and began pumping water into the galvanized wash tubs to do the 'wash.' When the tubs were filled, I added chlorine bleach to the water and watched as the water began to turn orange. I stirred it with the wooden paddle until the iron patches slowly settled to the bottom of the tub. The chlorine in the bleach extracted the iron from the water molecules and kept it from attaching to the fabrics. It also helped remove the stains I could not remove by rubbing.

The kids were still eating and playing around the kitchen table when I went inside to strip the beds of their sheets and pillow cases.

It bothered me to see the layer of dust on the bedroom floors. The floors were dusty because of the open windows and the dirt road in front of the house. It was almost impossible to keep them clean.

Clothes, which could have been clean or dirty were scattered across the floors in the bedrooms. I had to pick up each item and examine it before putting it in the pile with the dirty sheets.

Instead of the usual bungalow style, four room house, this one had an extra small bedroom squeezed between the front and back bedrooms. This gave Jim his own room. With each having a bed and a chest or dresser, I could not understand why their clothes were on the floor.

Our furniture, which we moved on a truck from place to place, consisted of a three piece bedroom set and two extra beds. Mom and Dad's bedroom had a bed and dresser from the set. Jim's room had his bed and the chest from the set. The room I shared with Nancy and Roy only had a bed. The kitchen table and chairs, our ice box, and kitchen stove were the only other furnishings in the house. The furniture had been with us for years and moved so many times that it looked ready for the junk yard.

I carried the dirty clothes out to the tubs. After putting the soap and linens into the tubs to soak, I pumped rinse water and went back into the house. Nancy and Roy had finished eating. I wet a cloth and wiped Roy's face. When I tried to wipe Nancy's face, she began kicking and screaming. As a matter of fact, she was becoming so difficult that I did not know what to do with her anymore. She was angry and touchy constantly.

I sent them off to play and returned to the laundry. I stirred the linens through the water. I raised them up and down trying to remove the dirt from the fields that stained them. The sheets were large and bulky, and being soaked with water, made them too heavy for me to raise them out of the wash water. So I put the scrub board down into the tub and lifted the sheets a bit at a time, rubbing each part of the sheet against the metal rub board.

The rub board had started to rust in places. I tried to avoid the sharp edges of the rusted out places, but whether it was the difficulty of handling the sheets or the magnitude of the job, or both, again and again, my knuckles scrapped across the open holes of the tin board, taking bits of my knuckles with each rub.

When I finished the rubbing, I twisted the sheets to wring out as much water as possible before dropping them into the bleach water, and then into the last rinse tub. They were still dripping when I carried them to the clothes line.

The clothes line was almost as high as I could reach. I had to throw the heavy sheets over the line to support the weight while I found the corners to pin them to the line. I was able to do this by securing two opposite corners of one end of the sheets. I then supported the weight by using more clothes pins to attach more of the sheet to the line as far as I could reach. I lifted the rest of the sheet off the line and ran my fingers along the edges, shaking and smoothing as I pinned. My arms were aching when I finished the first sheet. My stomach growled. With Nancy's outburst I had forgotten to see if there was any of the rice left. I would check after the sheets were hung.

The kids were still in the kitchen when I returned. The room had been somewhat warmed by the kitchen stove, which was the only heat in the house. While it was still warm during the day, the nights were becoming a bit chilly. The chill lingered through the house until mid-morning.

Looking at the clothing I had picked up from the bedroom floors, I knew it would take me past noon to get everything washed today. I hoped the sheets would be dry by the time I pumped the water and got the clothing washed.

It was past noon, maybe two o'clock, I had no way of knowing except by the sun, when I brought in the sheets and hung the other clothes to dry. I liked the smell of fresh, clean sheets on the bed. But the rest of the house was so stuffy and messy.

I began to gather other things from the floor. I tried to find places to put them away. The dresser and chest held some things in the two front bedrooms. But there was no place to put the rest, except back on the floor. So, I folded and stacked the rest, as neatly as possible, away from the walk space. In the back bedroom, I put everything in the far corner of the room across from the bed.

The bedroom still looked cluttered. So I took a clean sheet and covered the stack in the corner and folded the sides nicely. It almost looked like a chest covered with a scarf. And the room did not look quite as vacant.

We had an old broom made from straw. It had been used and worn down to a stub. Had the straws been longer, it may only have served as a whisk, fanning the dust from the floor into the air. That happened to some degree anyway as I tired my best to clean the floors. Eventually the bedrooms were as clean and straightened as I could make them. My arms ached from the washing and the sweeping.

Mother had not left any instructions. I did not know where they had gone or when they would be back. But the dishes were still dirty from breakfast and I knew they would have to be clean for dinner. I lit the gas burner of the stove and placed a filled kettle of water over the flame.

Having just come from the bedrooms and not finding the children in the kitchen, I looked into the empty living room. They were not there. They must have gone out to the front of the house.

The living room was never used. Our lifestyle was merely to work, eat, sleep, and repeat it day after day. Dinner and breakfast were mostly eaten by the light of the oil lamp. After eating, everyone went to bed or left for the day.

Other people in our extended family had furniture in this room. It was usually used for sitting and talking. And there were places for setting your coffee cup or to lay a book you were reading. If my family drank coffee, it was done in the kitchen. And there were no books in our house.

Some day I would like to have a living room full of beautiful furniture, I thought. Images played into my imagination. I began to place furniture in the room. Yes, this could be a beautiful room. I would place lace doilies on the back of the chair and on the armrests. Pictures would be on the walls and curtains at the windows.

The windows in this room were closed and dust from the yard and road clung to the panes making the room dark in spite of the light outside. And the large square card, telling the ice man what size block of ice to deliver, covered one of the window panes. But in my imagination, the room became beautiful and serviceable.

Coming back to reality, I began to clean the room from top to bottom. Even cobwebs were pulled from the ceiling and corners with a rag tied around the broom and stretched as far as my arms would reach. The kettle began to whistle.

I left my dreams behind and rushed back to the kitchen. I washed, rinsed, and stacked the dishes to air dry.

Mother would be so pleased when she returned today. I looked around me. The laundry was done, beds were made, dishes done, and the house cleaned. Maybe she would show me some appreciation. I always hoped. I had worked so hard. I was pleased. Mother had to be pleased also!

I heard Roy crying in the yard. No....screaming was more like it! Oh, Mother would kill me if I let something happen to the kids! I ran out the back door. Roy was standing with his left hand covering a rapidly swelling knot on his head. He also had his right arm across his face. His face was red and wet with tears. There was no doubt that he was in pain.

Nancy stood near by with sheer belligerence in her eyes.

"What have you done?" I ask her.

"She hit me with a stick," Roy whimpered.

"Why have you hurt your brother?" I ask.

"Because I wanted to," she replied and turned and ran into the house.

I examined the bump and put some cold water on it. I wiped his face until he quit crying. Then I held him in my arms and rocked him until he was ready to play again.

I went into the house to find Nancy to see if I could get the story from her before Mother came home. I would have explaining to do.

Nancy was not in the kitchen. I turned right to look into the bedroom. The bed was stripped and the clean sheets were lying on the floor. Nancy was not there. I raced to Jim's room. His sheets were on the floor. I raced on to Mother and Dad's room. The sheets were half on the bed and half on the floor. It looked as if Nancy had given the sheets a big yank as she ran past the bed. She had gone out the front door and across the yard to the field.

My heart skipped a beat. I knew Mother could be home any time, and now the beds were not ready. I had worked so hard. I was exhausted. I had not had anything to eat all day. I was upset and at my wits end with Nancy. But I knew she would come back when Mother came home. For now I had to get the beds done again.

I had started working first on Mom and Dad's bed when I heard the car drive up to the house. Panic overwhelmed me. Even without the beds completed, all my work, all my efforts, surely Mother could see!! I could explain to her about the beds! I had worked all day without a break! Surely, surely, Mother could see! I finished her bed with great care and went out to meet them in the kitchen.

"Where is dinner?" Mother demanded. (We were not able to eat everyday. I never knew whether to prepare beans or potatoes if they were in the house. It was Mother's job to spread out the food; to decide when it was to be eaten, over the week or a month, to make it last.)

"You didn't tell me if there was anything to fix when…" With pride I wanted to point out to Mother how much I had done.

"And look at those beds!" She screamed.

"Nancy did that." I said softly. "And I was fixing them when…" My words were cut off by the slap that had landed on my right ear. I stumbled back a step and received another one on the left side before I could balance myself again.

Mother was screaming and gritting her teeth at the same time. But I could not tell what she was screaming because of the ringing in my ears. And the blows continued, knocking me in one and then the other direction. I had remained within arms reach of Mother and her blows followed in rapid succession with stinging slaps across my face, eyes, and nose.

Her blows pounded my body as her anger mounted.

All the love and praise I had envisioned all day was met with this unbelievable outburst of anger and punishment.

I knew at that moment that there was no way of appeasing my mother. Nothing I could ever do would cause her to love me, or show me any kind of respect or concern. All the verbal and physical abuse I had taken from her had not brought my mother to any better handling of things.

Mother's behavior would never change, and would most probably continue to be even more unreasonable. All my love and effort toward catering to her wishes had been in vain.

And in that instant, a flood of emotion seemed to surge from the depth of me. An emotion, so strong, that it filled my entire being. My body became rigid as the emotion came from my stomach to my head. Was it anger? Was it hatred? I wasn't sure.

I only knew that as I stood there and looked at my mother, I was truthfully 'seeing' her for what she was. She was not a mother. She was a monster! She was a monster out to destroy me! Such loathing, I felt for both myself and her.

My eyes said to my mother, "This is the last time you will ever hurt me. I will not be your whipping post again." No words were spoken. But Mother stepped back, as if she had also been hit. She knew by the set jaw and the fire in my eyes, that the relationship between the two of us would never be the same.

I knew that as far as I was concerned my mother and I would never have a mother-daughter relationship. My mother was dead to me!!! In fact, how could I have believed that I had ever really had one? It just seemed that I had always wanted one, needed one. Now, I did not need a mother, or anyone. I knew that I could do better without one.

At that moment I could not understand why I had cared so much. All the little games I had played for Jim's and Mother's attention and approval blazed in my mind. Why did it take so long for me to accept the fact that they never had, and never would, care for me?

I was the servant. I was the whipping post. To feel good about themselves they only had to destroy something of value to me or beat on me.

But when they looked into my eyes that day they knew their behavior and actions would no longer work on me. My eyes, my body, became steel; not in the physical sense, but in an emotional sense.

If they were in a room, I would not be there if possible. Or, if for some reason I had to be there, my body would be turned away. I never looked at them. I never spoke. In my mind I was there without them being present. I had chosen to step out of their world, because I no longer 'needed' them in my world.

An interesting thing started to happen. I found I not only stopped paying attention to them, but I went for days (weeks, years?) without feeling anything. My mind reasoned through any thought or situation with cold indifference. Everything was calculated on the bases of logic without emotional input.

My mind and body became separate entities like what I had experienced at birth. My body became robotic. It performed as necessary. But, I gradually became aware that as my body performed, my 'mind-self' was somewhere else. I would find burns, cuts, scrapes on my body after performing the chores of cooking, washing, and cleaning. I did not feel them when it happened.

I instructed my body to be more careful.

Then there were times when my mind became bored or simply sought a connection with my body to reclaim the oneness of the physical and emotional self. The body continued to function as instructed by the mind, but the emotional self was not there to respond and interact.

My mind wasn't sure my emotions were still a functioning part of the whole. A neural connection, my mind reasoned, the emotional part of myself, had somehow shutdown. The one incident with my mother had overloaded the circuits and the fuses had been blown. No efforts from my consciousness could bring back an emotional reaction within my body.

That emotional aspect of my being was gone. Dead! There was a certain amount of peacefulness associated with that. My body and mind felt comfortable. My emotional pain was gone. To exist, I only had to do what was physically required of me.

Where my life had been emotionally unbearable, it was now filled with a fantasy world of books, pictures, and stories. It was a comfortable place with hopes of warmth, smiles, and a feeling of well-being. Yes, there was a place for me. I would find it someday. It would be waiting. But, I had to be here, endure, for now. I would show them I could make it without them, in spite of them! In my mind, the day to day things did not matter. Pain, cold, hunger, fatigue did not faze me. I continued, unceasingly, with whatever was required of me. I had been taught to keep quiet, unless spoken to. My world of silence became a world of refuge now. Whether my silence and indifference was interpreted as anger, or hatred, or something else, I did not know. Maybe my eyes said, "I dare you to hurt me again." If so, they did not care to challenge me too often. Then gradually they did not challenge me at all when they saw that their old tactics were not working on me. But where they had mistreated me before, I could now see how they looked right through me, and talked past me. I had been dispensable to them. I meant nothing to them before and it mattered little now.

In reality, I did have a part in the family's survival from crop to crop. I would only allow them to use me (I was still the slave. I just no longer allowed them to beat on me.) as long as it was to my benefit; until I was older and had other choices. I would have those choices someday.

Someday!

# 19

## The Good and the Bad

Spring - 1953

> *I had learned a valuable lesson. I would never fear hunger again.*

In the spring of 1953, I ended up in the latter part of the sixth grade in the Grey Ridge School District. All the sixth grade students were given a battery of tests.

Because of my test scores, I was named as an alternate to compete in English and social studies at the District Competition. I did not get to compete, but I was fortunate to be able to remain in the same district for another year. I actually attended the whole spring term of the sixth grade.

Even though I missed summer school and most of the winter months of my seventh grade year, I was there in the spring for the competition test. This time I outranked my competition and went to District to represent Grey Ridge seventh grade in English and social studies.

I did not win, but I did very well in social studies. After all, I had been reading and dreaming about the world around me and hungering to explore it.

I had even written a paper in the sixth grade called, "My Trip

### Zalora Price

Around the World." In it I told of every country, their capitols, major rivers, seaports (I traveled by ship), their products, social customs, and life style. I was preparing for my life to come.

 

The school year had not yet ended in my seventh grade year when things became very difficult for us. We were taken out of school because of another move. We now lived near my maternal Grandma and Grandpa and my Aunt Dot and Uncle Jay.

None of us in our families could not find enough work to feed our three families. In fact, the whole area was suffering. We had gone without food for a week.

Grandpa got word that Government Commodities were being given out the following Saturday at Salcedo store. The store was about five miles away.

In spite of the long walk, Daddy, Uncle Jay, and Grandpa were up early to walk to the store. They waited in line for hours. When they got to the front of the line, the only thing they had left to give to them was corn meal. Each of them received a five pound bag.

The women and children had waited with excitement all day. They were standing, watching for the men to come down the road. The children were so excited about the prospects of food that they had refused to find play activities to busy themselves.

Even though it had been nine days since I had eaten, my stomach had stopped hurting by the third day, what little it had hurt. I had put food out of my thoughts. I seemed to be able to control most of my body functions. I could eat, or not eat, sleep or not sleep, walk, run, work, to whatever lengths that I instructed my body. I had become an instrument of my mind. My mind became me. The body was simply a vehicle and not a very good one at that.

I think Mom and Aunt Dot had planned to go to them, to help carry the food the rest of the way home. But there were tears in their eyes when they looked and could not see any food.

They waited for the men to reach the house.

When they pulled the bags from their coats, the children

started hollering and grabbing at the bags. Dad let one of the children take his bag while he was trying to explain to Mom what had happened.

Before the adults knew what had happened, the children had ripped open the bag and were stuffing handfuls of dry cornmeal into their mouths.

There were outcries when Mother took the bag from them. She told them that she would have to cook some flap jacks.

The women put the seasoned, iron skillet on the stove. And after mixing water with the dry corn meal, and frying spoonfuls in the pan, they served hot flap jacks to everyone.

The three families lived off those three bags of corn meal for another two weeks; until cotton chopping time.

I learned a valuable lesson with this experience. I realized afterwards that there had been a small fear in me that the time would come when my family would either choose to not feed me at all, or they would be unable to provide the family with enough food and there simply would not be any left for me. Now I knew I would never fear hunger again. I knew that my strength and endurance may be challenged, but the fear had been erased. My catering to Mother and Jim had been out of fear as much as me trying to love them. The stress put on me, out of that fear, was no longer there. They had stopped beating on me, and if they stopped feeding me altogether it would take me a long time to die. I knew I could leave them and find food before I died since I had so much time to do so.

And a greater strength, one of personal power, caused me to stand back and observe the situation. Because of the deprivation I had to face, I knew that I had become stronger, would not succumb to momentary hardships, and was more determined than ever to have a better life.

# 20

## Day Hands

Harvest time - 1953

> *No one spoke of hopes, nor dreams; such would be folly.*

Daddy became increasingly unable to work because of his neck and back. Mother was not well because of her cancer surgeries. Jim and I were the only ones left in the family to earn a living. I was thirteen. He was fifteen.

Whenever possible, we made it into the fields. On those days, the mornings were cold. Unseen dew clung heavily to the rank, green leaves of the cotton in the twilight. Only a few feet of the rows were visible before the light of the rising sun showed over the horizon.

Life was hard and the laborers were quiet as they waited for sunrise. Most sat on their cotton sacks on the ground to preserve their energy. And a few milled around the wagons, which would be filled with cotton long before noon time. Their sunken eyes and thin muscular bodies indicated that most had only a bowl of rice for breakfast, and if they were lucky, they would also have a peanut butter, or baloney, with crackers for lunch.

Lunch would come late. There would be seven hours of labor before the sun shown from straight up in the sky. And another seven hours before the sun sank red and purple in the west.

But at three dollars per hundred pounds, the rank and heavy, dew laden cotton, would weigh in heavier for higher pay. It had to be picked before the sun dried away the moisture. Every ounce counted. So it was necessary that the heavy cotton be picked and weighed in before midmorning.

The chilly night air and frosty dew left the cotton not only wet but cold. Our fingers would be pricked over and over from the sharp burs. And we would have little feeling in our fingers because of the numbing effects of the cold. But, by midday, the frost would be gone, the cuticles bleeding, and the fingertips painful, crusty and split from the constant abuse.

There was little to say to each other as we sat around the wagon. We had been born into this life. Most would live and die in the same manner. No one spoke of hopes or dreams; such would be folly. We lived. We worked. We died. As sharecroppers and laborers, we worked the land, trusted in God for a good season, and had children. But I was speaking for them and not for myself.

I had had no breakfast. My stomach growled. My back and neck hurt before the day begin. My frail body completely rebelled to the chill, dampness and hunger. I felt light-headed. And even when the sack was full, it would take every ounce of reserve to hoist the end of the sack over my shoulders and carry it one-fourth to one-half mile to the scales.

Little by little, the 'life' seemed to be draining from me.

# Chapter 21

## Reassured

August - 1954

> *Incidents in our lives are invitations for opportunities.*

It wasn't enough for my family that my father had come home shell shocked and with shrapnel in his right shoulder and face from the war; that he had dived into shallow water and broken his neck and back which were wired together with copper wire, thus, leaving him physically and psychologically unable to work. Now my mother had been sent home from the hospital again after several surgeries…to die…they said. In the past four years they had cut all they felt they could cut and allow her to survive. Now her condition was serious and they could not cut more because she would die from the surgery. So they sent her home for the cancer to continue growing inside of her to be with her family until the end.

We had managed to get our thirty acres "share crop" planted in the spring. Jim was now hiring out at $5.00 a day by driving a tractor, plowing. And even though our crop was 'laid by,' there was still chopping that needed done to clear out cockleburs, jimson weeds, and cow vines. This was my responsibility as well as the housework.

The temperature gage showed 103 degrees when I picked up my hoe to return to the field. The cotton was rank near the house. It had grown higher than my head. Standing in it was smothering.

I chopped hard and fast in the dry dirt, breaking the dirt loose along the cotton row. I sometimes had to pull the larger weeds out by hand, gently, so as to not pull up any stalks of cotton. The stalks had already been thinned out, and what remained had to be left for producing the cotton.

The rows were one half mile long. I had worked my way to the middle of the field where the cotton came only to my waist. I chopped left-handed, then right-handed, to relieve the ache in my arms and shoulders. Blisters were stinging under the callousness that had already built up on my hands. The heat, pain and fatigue made me light headed. But the physical, I could endure. I would simply remove my mind and the body became merely a robot performing as expected.

My mind was a different matter! It worked lighting speed compared to my hands. I could not take away its determination.

My mind projected, as if on a screen in front of me, continued to play. It had a life of its own. It would not be silenced nor neglected. The body could work endless hours as required because it had been instructed to do so. My mind, on the other hand, constantly gathered information, sorted, analyzed, and stored; only to be retrieved, reworked, and making demands.

Suddenly, my mind had come to a conclusion! I was startled with its sudden clarity. It had reasoned that for fourteen years, this unit had been physically beaten, starved of food, love, proper clothing, and shelter, and labored with expectations beyond the resources of a child. And now with the medical condition of both parents, all hope was gone. More of the same difficulties and hardships would make it even harder, if not impossible, for me to reach the life I longed to have. As responsible as I felt, I knew I could not spend the rest of my life raising my mother's children in poverty. And there was nothing within my power to change things. Death would be better than surviving under these circumstances.

With the thought of death, came the thought of heaven and hell that my grandmother had taught in Sunday school class when I was ten years old. And there was a thought of the blue card hanging in our front room with God's Ten Commandments.

I was out of resources. But before I decided I would die, I remembered being told that God was supposed to have tremendous powers.

Then, not by choice, but by a logical conclusion of my mind, my voice went into automatic transmission.

"God!" I screamed. Pause.

"GOD!!!" The words were loud and demanding.

In that moment, a cylinder-like force surrounded me. I heard the sound and felt the pressure as it dropped down over my head.

I stood with both hands on the top of the hoe handle, leaning on it. Sweat ran down my bangs, and my braids stuck to the back of my neck. I pushed the worn straw hat back from my freckled face. I could see my brother on the tractor on the next field over. There was a dirt cloud around him and heat waves wiggled across the field behind him. I could see, but not hear, the tractor. I could not even hear or feel my heart beating. Total silence!

"Yes," came a reply; as if to bestow on me complete, undivided attention, and with a love that melted my heart.

At the same time there was no physical sensation of me having a body. I felt like a ball of consciousness that existed in the space of my body.

And in that moment, a plea came from my mind. "If you don't help me," I communicated, "I am not going to make it."

I knew that if my mind let go of my body that it would gladly succumb. And I was tired, so tired, of holding on to life.

"If my life has some significance to you, then it must also have some worth for me," I continued.

I wasn't quite aware at the time where my stance on fairness came from, but my plea for help went even further, into a bargaining position.

"If you will help me, I will make a pact with you," I said. There was never a doubt in my mind that I was talking to a very strong, loving force. For the first time, in a long time, there was no fear.

I had always been grateful for any thing in my short life and willing to give back in exchange for any consideration.

So, I continued, "If you will help me, then I will live my life for you. And I will do anything you ask of me. But, you must make my life worth living."

Those words came from the words of others in the Pentecostal church services I had attended, particularly, the part about 'living my life for him.' I wasn't entirely sure what that meant. I suppose I was asking for help from the only person who had been willing to listen and I wasn't going to let them get away without some incentive. And I had also been told that God never asks for us to do any wrong to ourselves nor others. This was important to me that I not cause the pain to others that I had been subjected to. Furthermore, I could not envision a life any worse that the one I had so I couldn't imagine worse things being required of me.

There was only a momentary pause after I finished my statement. I had the feeling that there was understanding there of what was in my heart as well as the intentions of the words being spoken. I didn't need to go on. No explanation was needed.

"Agreed."

Swish. The cylinder was lifted. I felt it go up as I had felt it come down. My senses returned. The sounds of the tractor and my breathing returned to my ears. The heat felt unbearable. And I watched as a white, fluffy cloud separate me from the sun, giving me shade. My mind was quiet. I had never known it to be so quiet. My body felt rejuvenated.

I worked until nightfall. I had never sung, but I even found myself humming a little tune when I returned to the house that evening.

In the weeks and months and years that followed, I seemed to always "know" within my being that the burden of life I had had to bear was now in God's hands. I sometimes wondered, later, what God might ask of me. But it was not a real concern. I knew it would not be anything more than I could handle.

Mother went back into the hospital for more surgery in the fall. She had regained some strength and they decided to take out more of the organs and surrounding tissue to get rid of any remaining cancer. She came home bedfast.

I continued with the cooking, cleaning, and laundry. Since Mother loved to cook, she tried to help. But she started hemorrhaging and had to be rushed back to the hospital.

I wish I could have felt some sympathy. But I felt nothing towards her.

# Chapter 22

## Welfare

> *They would rather die than ask for charity.*

With Mother ill and unable to help and Dad's back and neck in a very fragile condition, Jim and I continued to do the best we could. But even so, the few dollars we earned was not enough to feed the family from one pay check to the next.

The crops were finishing and we knew that before long there would be only the 'bolls' to pull in the cotton fields. The bolls were the unopened cotton that was left on the cotton stalks after the regular harvest. We were paid one dollar per one hundred pounds to strip the boles from the stalks. It was back breaking work and anyone with gloves wore them. Unfortunately, we had no gloves. Without protection from the spiny cotton burrs, our hands were seriously scratched and cut. Nevertheless, we would work the fields every day until there was nothing left to pull.

After about four weeks of constant labor, every field had been picked clean. So, with nothing else to do, I stayed home to take care of the laundry and to work around the house.

The day was very cold and windy. It was good to be inside for a change. I tidied up a bit as I gathered the accumulated dirty clothes for the laundry. The house was too small to set up my laundry tubs inside. So I had to do the laundry outside as usual.

## Deprivation Trauma

I reluctantly went outside into the near freezing temperature and pumped three tubs of water to wash the clothes. My Aunt Dot had an electric washing machine. But in our house every thing still had to be hand washed. Hand rubbing clothing and linens on the rubbing board and hand ringing them was a very time consuming and laborious job for me.

Denim jeans were the number one article of clothing on a farm. And ours were sweaty and dirty. They took a lot of rubbing.

By the time I had gotten the jeans done, I was so cold that I could hardly continue. I found myself standing in front of the clothes line and I had a pair of jeans that I was trying to pin on the line. I had thrown the pair over the line and had picked up a clothes pin to secure them. But my fingers were frozen. They were stiff and numb from the cold, and I could not release the pin. I went back to the tub and dipped my hands in the water to thaw them. I continued to hang each pair of jeans across the line, go dip my hands to thaw my fingers, and come back to the line to pin the jeans. I shook them and smoothed them. They hung on the line like sheets of ice.

I filled two of the lines with clothing before going back into the house.

When I came in the back door, I saw Mother talking to a woman in the front room. She had, somehow, gotten word to the Welfare Office that she wanted to talk with a welfare worker. Being ill, she could not work, and felt it necessary to go to any measure to feed the children.

Never, in our family, did 'children' include me. I also suspected that she was getting hungry herself because this was her first time to remain in the house without food to eat for an extended period of time, as she had done to me on a continuous basis over the years. Before her long months of illness she had always managed to go out and find food somewhere with family or friends.

I remained silent as she brought the woman into our kitchen. I heard her saying, "Our beans, flour, and lard are gone. I only have a handful of rice left, and the work has played out."

The woman looked around in disgust, gave a snort as if to get her nose above the smell of our kitchen which was always as clean as the surroundings would allow, and said, "There are able people in the family to work. I cannot help you."

She walked straight to the front door, and through it.

Mother stood there with tears in her eyes.

She and I had not spoken in two years, but I knew my family's position on welfare. They would rather die than ask for charity. She would rather have died first. But she was also the mother of three little ones and her own stomach was hurting. She could not stand by, letting them go hungry, without doing all she could do to feed them.

The welfare woman's rejection was both a hardship and a blessing. Now our family would never have the disgrace of taking charity. And no matter how painful, Mother had done her duty and reached out for help when there was nothing else she could do herself.

# Chapter 23

## Remembering

> *The deprivation of share croppers and day farm laborers was an accepted standard.*

By any standards my family would have been considered dysfunctional. But, on the other hand, every other family I knew was dysfunctional to some degree. Even the norm was not a healthy situation. That was the way things were. The deprivation of share croppers and day farm laborers was an accepted standard. We provided the backbone of farm production and received a hand to mouth existence. Starvation, physical abuse, verbal abuse, sexual abuse, lack of education, social rejection, and spiritual depletion were the norm for our existence.

We lived in shacks, using oil lamps, drinking cistern water collected from the rain, and maybe had some kind of bed for everyone to sleep on, and a table. Other things were optional. We existed.

The frustrations suffered by the parents were passed on to the children. Life was bewildering to most of them. And the only human being below the adults, in the pecking order of things, were their children.

My parents expected nothing more for us than they had for themselves. Yet, despite their lack of hope that this is all life held for me, I knew that I was only in this situation temporarily.

In retrospect, I can now see their struggles to survive, their own hopes and dreams unfulfilled, and their anger, bitterness, and even grief. And I would like to believe they were doing the best they could, with what they had to work with.

I feel sure my mother was doing the best she could for herself. Before and after her illness, she was gone from the home most of the time. She never told me where she was going or when she would be back. Basically, I took over her role in the home and she came and went as she pleased. I never felt she more that half tried to do the best she could for the (six) other children (not to include Jim) that she had, but never wanted.

Dad was present, but never really there. I do not remember any extended exchange of words with him from the age of five when he returned from the Army until I left home at the age of fifteen. He would at times, say, "Suzie" this, or "Suzie" that. All of the females in the family would turn. Whoever was the closest would oblige him. He never learned any of our names. He didn't want to know.

But, even today, I ask myself, "How can I condemn my father?" To use an analogy, I would have to agree that 'if his cup was full, more could not be added.' His cup was filled to overflowing with emotional icebergs before I was born into the family. He had suffered extensively in the war and with his health, and he could not emotionally handle more. I know he was always drawn to a simple life…one he could grasp and find peace of mind.

No matter how hard they tried, my father could not find peace of mind living with my mother. Her aggression was overwhelming to him. They talked of divorce constantly. Who is to say that his life was less difficult than mine?

# 24

## A New Life

> *My impatience with life was added to my list.*

My 'cotton field' experience gave me renewed hope and I began to expect more from life. I wish I could say that I was happier and that things got better. But in fact the hardship and confusion continued and my impatience with life was added to my list.

Life continued pretty much as usual. But underneath the surface of my life, little things began popping into my consciousness. These were interesting little things that I began to observe. The things that were happening could be summed up as coincidence. I sometimes felt led to a certain place, or into a certain situation. After paying attention and seeing how things in my life continued, time and time again, to work out, I began to trust that "leading." I concluded that there is no such thing as a coincidence. I realized the incidents in my life were invitations for opportunity and happened for a reason.

I knew I trusted myself to a higher power that had introduced itself to me in the cotton field, and that I was leaving myself open for growth and understanding. That growth and understanding did not always come easy for me. Most of my best lessons in life come from very difficult times in my life. In my life, if it was not a lesson, it was not difficult.

I held the distance between me and my mother and brother. But I found that beneath my cold unemotional exterior I still cared so much about everything happening in my family. I tended to hold on and try to fix things that were not under my control. Fighting for control and survival still became fearful for me at times. I came to realize that becoming fearful every time life offered me an opportunity to exercise my faith was not using my faith. To believe that God was going to help, if not entirely take care of things was exercising my faith. I just needed to combine my efforts with more faith and stop being fearful.

By the age of fifteen, I was looking for opportunities and wisdom in all situations whether I considered them 'good' or 'bad.' I had an 'understanding with God,' and I trusted there was a purpose in things. I no longer had to worry about survival.

I began to relax a little more and I 'knew' things were going to be okay for me.

At some point I began to flow with a feeling. That feeling presented itself daily to me. It was like a question in my mind demanding to be answered. At first, I would ask myself, "What is this I am feeling?" It seemed that in the midst of a thought or an action, my consciousness would be jolted into awareness. And I would feel uncomfortable and unsettled until I could get a sense of direction and a desire to move forward.

I would go through a series of questions. Somehow, within the questioning process, I settled upon a yes and no, question and answer routine that worked for me. These questions related to how I should proceed down life's pathway or what directions or choices I should make. Many times when I couldn't find the right question and continually got "no" answers, I would say that I did not know what I wanted, but I knew what I did not want. I had to proceed with the information I had.

The interesting thing, was the way my body told me which way was a "yes" and which way was a "no." The means of communication was only a 'feeling.' "Yes" was positive. "No" was negative. I do not know any other way to explain them. One said, "Go ahead." The other said, "Wait."

There was never a question in my mind concerning these feelings or their validity. They were part of me, and I assumed everyone operated on the same basis.

# 25

## A Look Back

> *There was nothing from mankind that I could ask for and expect to get.*

The ages of five to twelve years brought many changes in our family and my life. I never felt a sense of stability. There were the constant moves, fighting for survival, and the increase in size of the family.

With the new additions to the family came more and more responsibilities for me in caring for the children as well as the cooking, laundry, cleaning, and farm labor. I accepted them as my part of the responsibility to the family.

While Mother's beatings became increasingly worse, and I endured Jim's brutality, I still felt a part of the family; if only due to the fact that I was used. I had a responsible part in the overall functioning of our family. I was still not a part of Mother and Jim's lives. But I did have the younger children and I knew they needed me.

From birth I had been taught to not expect anything from anyone. That sense of independence carried over into those years. But, those childhood needs of wanting and needing love and attention, and approval remained with me in the end, even though I had thought myself numb to them during the worst of it.

Maybe by the time I was twelve, I still had nothing to lose by standing my ground with Mother and Jim's behavior. Maybe my consciousness told me that it was one thing to hurt me by omission (withholding food, love, etc.), and another thing to intentionally hurt me physically and emotionally by their brutality and harsh words.

The two years of silence (age 12-14) between me and the others was wonderful. I really think that if Mother had hit me again, that I would have hit her back. Jim could have really hurt me if I had done so, but I was beyond caring.

The time of reprieve from the physical and emotional abuse seemed to allow my consciousness to surface again. Consciousness brings the ability to see and understand the patterns of life. It allowed me to detach from things, whether they were people, attitudes, behavior, or even thoughts. I began looking at the larger picture of life. I became more aware of family dynamics in our home, even thought I would not, or could not, be emotionally responsive.

Everything continued the same in the family as before my rebellion, except Daddy. He had given some amount of attention to Nancy and Roy before his swimming accident. Now, after a few years, he seemed hardly connected to the family. I identified with him because both of us seemed to be on the perimeters of the family.

Even though I was on the outside looking in, it seemed at times that I was the only one doing or even considering what needed to be done. Maybe it was the lack of hope that did not allow them to see beyond the end of the season. My insistence on thinking, planning, and wanting to go to school, was not comprehended by anyone in the family. But life went on, and I played my role. I performed with dignity and pride. And my still, green eyes never wavered when challenged, mocked, or ignored. My family saw my strength, but never understood me any more than I had understood them at the age of three.

I began to wonder if they had abandoned me or had I abandoned them! At this point in time my emotional attachment was only to the younger children. My trust for food, shelter, and security had been erased since I could remember. They had failed me and now I had no need for them.

So, instead of concerning myself about getting approval and some semblance of love from my mother, my mind raced off to other things. I began tuning into my body again and paying attention to my mind. My body was fatigued, but it felt better than before, without the abuse. My mind wanted more; that same 'more' that it had been reaching for since birth.

Then, looking at the prospects of spending another twenty years raising my mother's children in poverty erased all the hope I could foresee.

My body was tired, and my mind had become weary. I had to find a reason to hope. There was nothing from mankind that I could ask for and expect to get. So the only thing left was a higher power. I had not consciously considered that source until the moment it happened. And I was extremely surprised when I got an answer! Maybe I was too young and naive to question that interaction with 'God.' I did not have anyone to share it with, and therefore, no one to cause me to doubt it had happened. And this was all good, because the Universal Mind, the Creative Intelligence, the Divine Wisdom, that Cosmic Consciousness, has been a part of my life ever since.

# 26

## Something Has Got To Give

November - 1954

> *More than anyone, Mother taught me what it took to survive, even though her priorities were different from mine.*

I don't know if the spring draw (usually twenty dollars a month from December to May, to feed us until we could work in the fields) was repaid in full. I only know at the end of the season, it was time to pick up and move again, with nothing to show for our labor. Dick King, who owned the land we farmed near Sikeston, Missouri, was probably experienced enough with share-croppers to know that it wasn't going to get any better with two kids doing the farming, no matter how much heart we put into it.

There was still a little day work in the area when we arrived on Dewey Thompson's place on Nigger Wool Swamp, about fifty miles from our previous address. I hated the name. But it was a common name during the fifties. Even more, I hated the reason it was called that. It was said that so many Negros were killed and thrown into the water that their hair floated on the water and on the banks. Many were supposedly killed at a local night club by other Negro. I supposed that prejudice caused a few deaths as well.

But November came with the winter rain, wind, and freezing. We had a half-mile of knee deep mud along the ditch, in front of our house, before reaching a back road. The road was trailed with deep ruts and waterholes that required knee high boots for crossing. And without coats, boots, and even proper underwear, the best we could do was to spend a greater part of our days huddled close to the wood stove.

I asked about going back to school.

Mother flat out said, "No!"

She said that there was too much work to do. After all, she had three small children for me to take care of, housework, cooking, laundry, etc.

Jim and Dad were finding a little work, and I felt that I had to do my fair share. I continued the housework and on a few sunny days, we took our cotton sacks to the fields to pull bolls.

I was lucky if I could pull one hundred pounds of bolls a day. My nine foot sack would become wet and muddy from the water and ice on the ground. The weight alone was a burden for me. But I tackled the cotton bolls like everything else in my life; with as much vigor as possible.

My frozen fingers bled from the burr scratches and jabs. Numbness filled my whole body due to the lack of proper clothing. We had to keep moving to keep up our circulation.

"Just a few more feet," became a reminder that every pound bought a few more beans. And the beans meant survival!

With the spring thaw came hopes of returning to school. But, Mother said, "There is no need to discuss it, until after the crops are in the ground."

I had been warned with that cold look that only she could give. I had asked and complained so many times about going back to school. She did not want to hear of it any more.

I stayed quiet until May 1$^{st}$. Since it was customary to have the crops in the ground by May first, our crops were in. And there were three more weeks until school was out at Lilbourn High School. They had less of a farm community than the other locations we had lived. Their school year ran September through May.

She had run out of legitimate excuses. She was doing well with her health and there was no work to be done until the cotton came up and was ready to chop. Reluctantly, Mother agreed to get me to the school in Lilbourn, Missouri, to see what we could do about getting me back in school. She knew I wanted to be able to start high school in the fall.

Mr. Taul, the principal, took one look at us, and told us flatly that he saw no need to start to class this late. No, he would not allow me to take the State Examination for the eighth grade, because I had not been in school since my seventh grade year. I could come back next year and take the eighth grade.

I had turned fifteen in March and I did not want to come back to school at Lilburn High and be in the eighth grade at sixteen years of age.

That did not concern Mother who stated more than once that she expected me to be married by the time I was eighteen, implying that there was no need for an education to get married. We returned home. She was quite satisfied that she had done her fair share for me. She gave me her look that said, "Are you satisfied now?" I walked away searching through my mind for ideas. My mind was screaming inside my head that I would never be satisfied until I got out of the poverty.

A few days later, I rummaged through the house looking for a dress. I had only worn Jim's hand-me-downs for years. Now, at fifteen, I stood taller than Mother. But her dresses were also not right for me. So, I put a change of clothing (shirt and jeans) into a brown paper bag. I was looking for socks.

"What are you doing?" Mother asked.

"I am going back to Grey Ridge to talk to Mr. Rashe, the principal, there." I replied.

"That's fifty miles!" She exclaimed.

"I know." "I'll walk, but see if I can get a ride." I responded.

"Why can't you leave it alone?" She demanded.

"I want to go to school." I replied more strongly than I expected! In a more controlled voice I continued, "I went sixth and seventh grade there, and Mr. Rashe knows me. He will remember me representing the school in the district competition in English and Social Studies. Maybe he will let me graduate eighth grade."

With that, I continued my preparation for leaving.

"Okay." It had taken her a while.

"Give me a day, and I will see if I can find us some transportation. And I will go with you. Anything could happen to you, out on the road by yourself."

I almost laughed. She had been willing to emotionally deprive me, starve me, and beat me to death, but she did not want someone else to hurt me.

But, then, she was also big on appearances.

With brown bag in hand, I crawled into the front seat of a borrowed, beat-up truck.

Resourceful, Mother was! I appreciated her for that. More than anyone, she taught me what it took to survive, even though her priorities were different from mine.

Mr. Rashe was pleasant to talk with. Yes, there were only two weeks left of school. Yes, I could enroll today; attend classes until the state exam was given. As an enrolled student, I could take the exam with everyone else. If I passed, I could go on to high school.

"Yes!"

After filling out some enrollment papers we headed out of town to the country in the old battered pickup. There were miles and miles of cotton and soy bean fields. But being miles and miles from nowhere, we were still on the Gray Ridge school bus route where I needed to be, to catch the bus to go to school.

We went first to Grandma Barnes' house. "Yes, she can stay with us," she said after we filled her in on our plans. Shirley Jean, her youngest child was married. It was just her and Grandpa.

I had one major concern about taking the state exam. I had missed out so much on math, especially algebra. Aunt Dot, who lived down the road, was the only one in the family who had made it to the eighth grade. She had learned some algebra.

Our next trip was to talk with her. She had four children younger than me. She said if I would not press her when she was busy that she would teach me what she knew. I was ecstatic.

I waved down the school bus on the first day and told the driver that I would be there to be picked up each day until the end of school. It made no difference to him. He nodded and I found a seat. Several small children stared at me.

I knew the school from my attendance in the sixth and seventh grades. I found the classroom down the hall from my old seventh grade room. I peeked into the classrooms on my way down the hall to see if any of my old teachers where still there. I saw one and made a mental note to go see her later.

My classroom was crowded. There were no books for me and they had to locate a desk for me to use. It was put in the farthest space in the back of the room.

It was a strange situation and unlike the classes I had attended before. I arrived each morning on the bus, sat in the classroom, and went home on the bus in the afternoon. There was nothing neither expected nor required of me.

The teacher did not bother to include me in the classes. After all, I did not have a transcript to follow me because I had not attended school for the past year and a half. She must have felt that there was no way I could pass the exam even if she included me. It didn't matter because semester test were being given and I was not allowed to take them because I had not covered the material. And the last few days were taken up by turning in the text book and library books. The students in the classroom looked at me with curiosity. But since the teacher did not include me, they didn't either.

The examination day arrived the week before school ended. They sat us in the auditorium for the test. It was a timed exam. All the seats were double spaced so we could not look on the paper of someone else.

I finished and turned the exam paper over on top of my desk, and waited until time was called. I felt I had done well.

The days that followed the test were true mental anguish for me. My whole life was attached to the test score.

Then the grades and rank were posted a week later. I approached the board and a few of the students stared at me and stepped aside to give me space to stand in front of the board. There had been ninety-two students taking the exam. I read down the list. Fay Johnson ranked #6 in class. Only five others had done better than me. I was going to graduate!!!

Mother said she would come. And she did come.

She not only came, she brought me a graduation dress. It was the first store bought dress I could remember ever having. It was a light gold taffeta, with an organza overskirt with flocked daisies. And it had a blue satin ribbon for a belt. The dress looked like it was a dress for a young child. It was a bit small for me and quite snug across the breast. I did not comment, because the graduation gown would cover the dress.

It was the first thing she had ever done for me without me asking that I could ever remember. Secretly, I questioned her motives. I could not believe that she would do something specifically for me. And it was altogether possible that Grandma told her that I needed a dress for the graduation. I don't think it would have occurred to her.

I do not know where she got the dress or the money for it. But, she was there taking full credit for the occasion. She was very pleased with herself for going to such great lengths to help me with my education! She told everyone how she had made such an effort to keep me in school.

Graduation was over. We had returned to Grandpa and Grandma's house for the night.

I felt restless, ready to move on! And I wandered aimlessly that morning through the house, waiting for Mother and Grandma to visit before our trip back to the ditch bank along Nigger Wool Swamp.

Passing through the small alcove that separated the living room from the bedrooms was a small, linen-type closet, with open shelves. Peeking out from underneath a stack of bedding, was a bit of white eyelet lace.

Lace of any kind was rare on the farm. My blooming femininity was captivated. Yet, the ground rule of our community was to bother nothing that belonged to another person.

My feet carried me to and fro along the hallway as my mind contemplated the piece of lace and its attachment to…a yet unknown garment?, or maybe a table scarf?, or…?

"What are you doing Fay?" I heard my mother's voice say.

My constant movement had caught her attention. My hand had reached unconsciously, to see what the lace was attached to.

"I wanted to see what this is attached to." I said.

I pulled slightly on the item to show her what I was referring to. In doing so, I caused a stack of linens to fall, revealing a garment made of a beautiful, soft material, in colors of pinks, grey, and tan. The fabric was store bought and not material from a feed or flour sack.

The lace was about one-half inch wide and attached to a white yoke that ran from sleeve to sleeve. There was a square neckline and a gathered bodice underneath, attached to a full, gathered skirt.

"That's just a little dress I made for Shirley Jean." Grandma said. "It's too little for her now. You might be able to wear it."

My heart pounded. "A dress, with lace, for me?"

"Go try it on if you like it." She continued.

Mother nodded her head, giving her approval.

Before I could gather up the dress, Grandma said, "You have grown so much, Fay. I think she might have another dress that you can have, if you want it." She had not offered them the two weeks before. She must have decided that I deserved them now that I had graduated the eighth grade.

I eagerly followed her into the bedroom.

She went to a drawer and pulled out another dress. It had a sheath body and a pendulum to go around the waist. She spread it on the bed for me to see. I stared at the two, side by side. They were beautiful! They were grown-up! These soon would be mine!

When I stepped into the living room in the slim-fitting sheath dress, Mother gave me a startled look. She had not even noticed that the taffeta organza graduation dress had not fit me. It had been a girl size and I was certainly a Misses size now. And I stood a good four inches taller than Mother.

# 27

## Coming of Age

August - 1955

> *I made a vow to myself that my life would be what "I" made it. I knew what I did not want.*

Why wasn't I surprised?

"I don't see how you can talk about going to school. We don't have the money to send you to school," was her only comment.

Interpreted, this meant, 'we must buy Jim new clothes and his discards are not fit to be worn in public.'

But what she refused to acknowledge was that Jim's hand-me-downs were no longer going to fit my clothing needs. I had been small and slow to develop because of the poor nutrition. But now at the age of fifteen, the changes in my body were showing. When we began removing the layers of clothing in early summer, I noticed more changes. My thighs were round and my buttocks now hid my boney frame. The knots had gone away in my breast and the fullness was soft.

Intrigued with my new developments, I wanted to see what I would look like in one of Mother's dresses. I rummaged through the scattered clothing in the bedroom and came out with one that she had not worn for a while. I slid the dress over my head. It fit!

Well, almost! A little more fullness up front would help.

Throughout the summer, I wore a few of Mother's cotton dresses during the day, when I was working around the house. She had several hand-me-downs that she did not like. It was on such a day when Dewey Thompson stopped by to offer some day work. Mother, Dad, and Jim were gone.

"There's no one here but us kids," I said.

"Us kids," he replied, stressing the word 'us.' The look in his eyes told me even more as his eyes went down and then back up my body. I KNEW what he meant, but I was not interested. I had decided that sex and babies were not for me. The, blank, unknowing look I put on my face told him more than words could have said. Since I did not respond to his awareness of my body and the implication that I was now an adult, he dropped the conversation. I knew in that respect things were going to be different and I had to stop thinking of myself as one of the kids and remember that I was a blossoming young woman.

That day, I made a stronger vow to myself that my life was going to be what "I" made it. While I did not know at that moment what I wanted, I knew what I did not want! That was more of the same that I had had for all my life. I knew that sex makes children. I did not want children. I did not want hunger. I did not want to be cold. Sex and marriage meant all of these things to me. And I would have neither! I was going back to school...my only way out!

# 28

## Time to Move On

> *My timing...or that of the Universe?*

It was after Mother had said that the family could no longer support me in my goal for an education that I put on a hand-me-down dress from my aunt, put on a coat I found crumbled in the floor, and put my saddle oxfords and socks in a brown, paper bag. I don't remember if the shoes were hand-me-downs or from a church rummage sale. They were functional and that was what mattered. I started out for Lilbourn, Missouri. I spoke to no one about my plans.

I arrived two and a half hours later; cold, wet, and with mud up to my knees.

There was an old gentleman sitting on a Pepsi-cola crate in front of a service station, just at the beginning of the main street of town. He watched me closely as I approached him. He was aware of the mud on me and the bag in my hand. I am sure he was trying to figure out where I had come from, and why I was walking across country alone in my bare feet on a cold day. I looked at the ground and asked shyly if I could use the rest room on the back of the building.

"Sure, little girly. You go right ahead." He motioned towards the restroom door.

I glanced up at him and saw a typical, small town looking

man that was rough around the edges. The look in his eyes said 'a gambling man.' Then I saw it. A little dance of light around him. "Um-m," I thought. There is more depth to this man than meets the eye.

Comfortable with this man and his gas station, I followed his gesture towards the 'restroom' sign above a door on the back side of the building. The temperature inside the room was colder than the outside. A pull chain light bulb was hanging from the ceiling. I pulled on the chain. A dull light bulb cast shadows in the room when I closed the door. The facet made a grinding sound when I turned on the water. It was cold. Putting one foot at a time into the sink, I washed the mud from my feet and legs.

The droplets of cold water clung to my skin causing goose bumps on my legs. My hands had also turned red from the cold. I patted my legs and feet to dry up some of the moisture. They were still damp when I put on my socks and shoes.

I put everything back exactly as I had found it. I thanked him as I passed by him on my way up the street.

I could feel him watching me as I went from store to store. I went into every business asking for a job. I covered both sides of the street as I went. And I had almost reached the end of the street when I came to Jones Rexall Drugstore.

Joy Jones was a pretty lady. She moved with a slowness of purpose that never out staged her feminine quality.

Her husband, Bill, had purchased the store from Mr. Castleberry about two years earlier. But for a year now, Bill had suffered from emphysema, and was recuperating at home.

Joy was not comfortable in her role as overseer and clerk. And she suffered the soda fountain with the greatest amount of indignity. In fact, she had recently spoken to Bill about getting some additional help at the fountain in the afternoons, when the school crowd showed up.

Now I presented myself as a solution to the problem.

I was not exactly what Joy had envisioned. But there was no

doubt that I needed a job.

In my mind, I could learn to do anything. And my eagerness was obvious!

In the back of her mind she was probably thinking that if they took the time to train me that (as I needed the money) I would stay on the job for a while and they would not have to keep training replacements. So, the general inclination was to hire me since it was obvious from looking at me that I needed the money.

It seemed that my timing was right. My timing…or that of the Universe? I returned home with excitement in my heart that I could now pay for my own education. The miles of walking and the cold could not dampen my spirit.

School started and the bus came within a mile of the ditch bank where we lived, to pick us up for school. Only I had another problem. We lived another half mile further down the ditch from the bus turnaround. That mile and a half I had to wade through the mud tracks and water to the bus stop. And I had to go straight to the school restroom and clean up before classes. But, I was in school. That was all that mattered.

Jim should have been in the tenth grade. But he did not return to school.

Joy and Bill had decided to try me out by scheduling me to work three nights a week. Those three nights a week I went straight to the store after school. I practically ran to beat the after school rush, because some of them had automobiles. I worked from about 3:00 pm in the afternoon to 10:30 pm at night. The store actually closed around 10:00 pm but I had to take down the custard machine, clean and lubricate it, to have it ready for the next day. All the glassware, mixers, blenders, and silverware had to be washed and sterilized for the next day also. So, on week nights it could easily be 10:30 pm when we left the store.

Jim surprised me by showing up to walk home with me a few times. I think he also needed an excuse to get off the farm. This happened when I least expected it, and it greatly pleased me.

**Zalora Price**

The five mile walk home from town was long and tiring. We did not talk. But, then, we never had.

# 29

## My First Job

> *I was at the bottom of the economic ladder. I was invisible to them.*

My job had begun at the Drugstore.

I felt like a robot. I WAS a robot! One with long, flaming red hair and intense green eyes. I was very thin, and covered with freckles.

I stood behind the soda fountain watching the young people in the booths chattering, laughing, and making plans. Others were taking turns playing the pin-ball machine beside the front door.

Those sitting across the fountain on the barstools were talking about their worlds.

And at that moment I 'knew' and almost thought out loud, that nobody can become a human being alone. We need love and attention and training from relationships, whether it is from family, friends, or community. These young people surrounding me had experienced all three. I had had none.

In the following months, loneliness ached in my heart and I thought I would go mad because of the isolation. I did not know how to interact. My family had not given me enough social contact to know how to interact and feel socially acceptable.

During all my years in grade school, I had come to know that 'culture' formulates all of our existence, as an expression of economics. I was at the bottom of the economic ladder. I was invisible to them.

But I had to finish high school. I would be invisible if necessary to finish school. That was my goal, and nothing would cause me to loose sight of that goal. I had strengthened my resolve to get an education and pull myself out of the poverty cycle.

I had made it for fifteen years. I could and I would make it for more. No matter what I must suffer.

And I was suffering in a way that I could never have imagined. The other young people's world was so different from mine. I knew I would never put my trust or my hopes in any of them. I neither wanted nor needed them in my life. Their world seemed as abstract to me as mine would have to them. They would slow me down if I invested my energy into becoming a part of their world.

I decided that I would watch and take mental notes. They might come in handy one day.

I knew there was something else waiting for me beyond high school. This was not it.

I also knew that I had some personal preparation to do for survival in social situations. I needed survival skills for the totally new situation of working in the public. I also needed coping skills to survive.

As a matter of preparation I began to compose situations, behaviors, attitudes, circumstances, etc. and reasoned how, when, and why things happened in the social milieu I had encountered. If I were to win at the game of life, I knew that I had to anticipate and be one step ahead of everyone else in the game.

Deciding who the players were at any given time became a constant and very important part of the 'game.'

I started to make judgment calls. If my judgment was not good about a person or situation, I would reflect on what went wrong. From there my mind became abstract in its analysis. I would pull bits and pieces out of a scenario to see how the game would play out if I did this or did that. From this I would generalize and imagine alternative outcomes.

I think I could say my mind was constantly alert. But it was more than alert. It was instantaneously responsive. If I were not sleeping, my mind was processing everything within distance of my six senses. (That's my five physical ones plus my intuition.)

I was fearful and anxious about the environment I had encountered. But being new, it was interesting as well.

I was certainly 'all in my head.' Keeping my logic separate from my emotions brought me physical survival, but also loneliness, and a feeling of being empty in heart and spirit in this new crowd.

From deep down in my being, I felt the anger grow and I pushed it down, down, down, as far from my consciousness as I could. Out of my anger I demanded to know from the universe why I had been born to live in the difficult existence given me.

From the far reaches of my mind came the 'knowing' that whispered, "Someday". Someday I would not feel lost, abandoned, and outcast.

The weather became increasingly cold and wet during the following winter months. Joy delivered a baby boy. Bill returned to work part time in the pharmacy. I was asked to work everyday after school and Saturdays and Sundays.

My friend would nod to me from the Pepsi-Cola crate from the front of the service station each weekend day when I arrived to clean myself and put on my shoes and socks, before proceeding up the street to the drug store.

It would sometimes take hours before I got 'feeling' back into my face, hands, and knees after walking to work on the weekends in the freezing weather. It slowed me down at work. And it was painful.

Maybe it was the thought of the pain, maybe something else that brought me to ask the girl across the table at study hall if she knew of any place I could get a room in town. She said 'no' but she returned the next day with a proposition. It was one that I could handle.

Her name was Elizabeth Higgons. She lived with her mother and three younger siblings. Her father had been shot and killed in an accident. Her mother was ill, and they could use some extra money. I would have to sleep with Elizabeth and her sister (three to a bed). And they would let me sleep with them for two dollars and fifty cents a week. This did not include food. But that would work! It would leave me enough money for school supplies and lunches, and enough left to help keep my brother and sisters in school with shoes and lunches.

So that winter of 1955-56 passed. Daddy got a small veterans pension started. It was for only twenty dollars a month. But that was enough to rent a house on Lilbourn's North Project.

Lilbourn had two Projects. The South Project was for Lilbourn's Negro population. The North Project was for poor white folk.

The twenty dollars a month got us a run down wood frame house and an outdoor toilet with its wasps and spiders. There was a water pump in the back yard. And it also had a line running to the kitchen. But the pump in the kitchen was difficult to prime and we carried water from the back.

Each of our moves had meant piling our bedding and kitchen things into a borrowed pickup truck. The family could bring these things, but to move into town, I wanted the living room furniture I had dreamed of having. I wanted a home like others I had seen.

Bill Mitchem's Furniture Store sat across the street to the right of Jones Rexall Drugs. I could see the furniture in the windows. I watched them loading furniture for delivery, from the drug store window across the street when I would look out.

Living at home would leave me the extra ten to twelve dollars a month I had paid Mrs. Higgons. I decided to talk with Mr. Mitchem.

As it turned out, he was pleased to give me credit on a living room suite. I selected a set with a sofa, a chair, three tables, and two lamps. I also arranged to have linoleum put down on the rough wood floor. I was given thirty-six months to pay.

The floor covering was laid. The furniture was delivered. And, when I added lace curtains to the windows, I felt like I had just walked into my dreams.

The family moved in. Jim had a job working nights at the

all night truck stop on Highway 62 at Howardville, Missouri. Mother had a job working at the Palace Restaurant up the street from the drug store.

For a while things were looking up. I walked the kids to school, went on to my school, and walked to work in the afternoons and on weekends.

It was on a Saturday afternoon that Bill Dillard walked into the drug store. He was the owner who had hired Mother to work at the Palace Restaurant. When he walked out the door of the drug store that day, my eyes followed him to the curb. A black coffin appeared and rolled across the street. Bill Dillard reappeared in its place on the other side. And I watched him walk to the liquor store just past Mitchem's Furniture. I knew at that moment that he was going to die. It did not bother me. I did not know him personally. The information flowed past me, as so much other information that my mind processed.

Bill Dillard died at 2:00 am the next morning of a heart attack. The restaurant was closed.

Without a job, Mother decided to open her own place out on the highway, at the intersection of Highway 60 and 62. It was an all night truck stop, and a successful venture. Not only did she make a little profit, she also met Joe Johnson.

She was in love. This was not an affair type thing. This was the 'love of her life.' Her feelings for him were so strong and forceful; she could only flow with it. And that flow took her to St. Louis, Missouri with Joe Johnson to find work and to make a life for them.

When Dad got the news, he cried on my shoulders for a week. When he was cried out, he proclaimed to me, "Since she has left us I, sure as hell, am not going to take care of her dammed kids." And the next day he was gone also.

The kids had been dumped on me since Frances had married. I supposed they both thought that I would carry on as usual. And I did. Doing the best that I could.

## Deprivation Trauma

I later learned that Dad had moved in with his sister and her children. He was working some. And he let me keep the veterans check for the rent for a couple of months.

Caring for the children and getting them to school was manageable until summer came. When school was out and I worked for twelve hours a day (8:00 am - 10:00 pm), the children could run free. I worried constantly about them. But all I could do was work to feed them and put a roof over their heads. I hoped upon hope that they had the same survival skills that I had and could take care of themselves.

# 30

## He Got His Revenge

> *I had other choices in this matter.*

Mr. Taul, the high school principal, was not a bit pleased when I showed up with my eighth grade diploma, to register for the ninth grade. He took it as an offense against him that I had the gall to go around him and come back there for the ninth grade after he had forbid me to do so.

For a year, he would stand where I could see him in the hall at school, and glare at me when I passed. He and his sister also ate their dinner at Lillie Mae Cole's diner, next door to the drug store where I took my breaks and ate when I could. When passing, he would lift his chin, grunt, and pass by me without speaking. His behavior spoke loudly, "I don't like you."

Then my tenth grade year, he was able to get even. I had finished General Math during my ninth grade year. The schedule called for me to take Algebra 1, my tenth grade year. This was a course that he taught. I wasn't any happier about being there than he was to have me in the class. But at that point neither of us had any choice.

After the first six weeks, he called me into his office.

"You are not doing well," he told me.

"All my test scores have been good," I responded.

"Well, that might be…" and he paused.

"The fact of the matter is...you have not turned in all of your daily homework."

That was true. With thirty-five hours a week in school, for classes, fifty hours a week at the drugstore, walking to and from each, and my other duties and responsibilities at home taking care of the younger ones, there was just not enough time in my schedule to do all the little "busy work" assignments that were handed out. It was easy for me to grasp concepts, commit to memory anything said in class, and review for the text before an exam, but anything else was almost impossible for me to handle.

"Your homework counts for half your grade. Since you have not done your homework, I am going to have to fail you."

I stared at him. I understood the game. He knew I understood his little game. There was a little smile of satisfaction that crossed his face.

"Now," he continued, "If you will just sign this paper, saying you wish to drop my class, I think I can give you an "Incomplete" instead of an "F." There was that 'gotcha' smile again.

Dropping Algebra meant that I could not take any advanced math courses, including Geometry and Trig. I could not take Chemistry. These courses had Algebra as a prerequisite. But, I also knew that my body was being pushed to its limits. I did not know if I could take an extra hour each night of the week for the homework assignments, which was the only way I could fight him. And what was there to say that he might also find some other way to get back at me. He had the upper hand, and if he wanted to fail me, he would find another way.

I signed the paper and walked out the door. I refused to look at him or give him any further satisfaction.

It was a difficult decision for me. And I was angry. He was playing a game that affected my life and my future!

But then he was not the first person who had stood in the way of my education. His behavior just made me even more determined to get where I was going. I had other choices in this matter. I could go over him or around him. I did not have to go through him to get educated.

I saw him often. I never spoke to him, nor did he speak to me, for the rest of my high school days. He would look at me as if to say, "I guess I sealed your college plans." And when our senior year came, he was very busy writing letters of recommendation to send off to Universities with other student's transcripts. I think he almost wished I had asked him to write a letter for me, just so he could decline. I would not give him that satisfaction.

# 31

## Mother Returns

> *I didn't trust her. She had abandoned us before.*

The phone rang loud and long.

The customers looked aggravated seeing that I was the only one available to answer it. They waited as I picked up the receiver, and looked away, absent mindedly, trying to fill the moment.

I had never talked on a telephone before coming to work at the drugstore. And I still did not feel comfortable answering the phone.

"Jones's Rexall Drugstore," I answered.

"Fay?"

"Yes."

"This is Mom."

"Oh."

"We're in town."

"Are you coming to see me?" I asked.

It had been a long time, actually several months, without my parents. Jim had left soon after them. I had struggled on. I had had a great deal of anxiety over the many decisions I had to make. And there was no one to talk with about those choices and final decisions.

"Uh…no. We are here, that's Joe and I. We are on our way to

Illinois. We don't have enough time. We wanted to take the kids and some furniture. If that is okay?"

"Yes, okay," I replied. Disappointed.

"You gonna be alright?" she asked. She must have caught something in my voice.

"Yes…Where are you going?" I wanted to know where she was taking the children. I didn't trust her. She had abandoned us before. She might do it again.

"We don't have an address yet. But a fellow Joe knows, Red Kurley, in Alto Pass, Illinois has a place on his property he said we could have. (It turned out to be his hen house.) I'll let you hear from me."

"Okay," I acknowledged.

"Well, bye." She ended the conversation.

"Bye."

All afternoon, my mind kept drifting back to the children. Katie hardly remembered her mother. Nancy at fourteen was hard to handle, and Roy was coming under the influence of some of the boys in the neighborhood. With me working fifty hours a week, plus the regular school day since my 11th grade year had started, the children were not getting the supervision they needed. Maybe it was for the best.

I was exhausted when the store was closed and locked behind me at 10:50 pm. It had been a hard day. Now I had the mile and a half walk home to the Project. The walk was like a winding down period for me.

It was late September and the nights had become cold. The first frost could come as early as October this year. I adjusted my car coat and my school books pressed a large button into my breast. The popular saddle oxfords and bobby socks were well suited for the distance I had to tread each day by foot.

High corn stalks stood between eight and ten feet tall on both sides of the dirt road. It was a little unnerving to leave the town street lights and walk alone in the dark. The sky was overcast and I couldn't see in the darkness. I walked quietly, and I hoped that I would be able to hear any movement that would alert me to run, if the need arose.

Now the Project was in front of me. Some lights were still on. I walked on, to the far end of my street.

The emptiness hit me even before I arrived at the house. It, somehow, even felt different from the yard. Climbing on to the small front porch, I reached for the screen door. The sound seemed to echo through the silent night. Opening the front door, I felt for the light switch, just inside. The light bulb hanging in the middle of the room exposed a barren, vacant room. Even the curtains and blinds were gone!

Startled, I raced to the bedrooms and kitchen. Every thing was gone! Everything except my bed frame and wire coil springs. And there, left behind, was my small four drawer chest that Uncle Jay had made for me before he died. My socks and underwear were still inside the chest. And my other two dresses still hung on the nail on the wall.

Somehow, the empty house seemed colder than the wind that had blown around me during my walk home. My mind drifted to the heating stove which was no longer there. The cold, empty house no longer had warmth from heat nor loving faces. I felt as empty and cold as the house. For the first time in my life, physically, I was totally alone.

Closing the bedroom door, I unzipped the hood of my car coat. Lying down on my back, I spread the hood under my head and pulled the coat tightly around me. Then I adjusted myself on the hard, cold metal coils of the springs as I closed my eyes and fell into an exhausted sleep.

# 32

## Taken in from the Cold

November - 1957

> *There exploded in my head a profound realization. I am more than my body.*

The walks home after work, to an empty house, became increasingly difficult. September rolled into November. The north wind blew against my legs, and my knees were frozen, red, and numb by the time I reached the cold, dark, empty house.

I feared that others learning that I was living alone, would try to abuse me. I was female, wasn't I? They could be waiting for me and attack me in the darkness. They might physically and sexually attack me, and maybe even kill me to hide the crime. I now had a different kind of survival to worry about.

Few people were out and around town these days. They ran in and out of the stores to grab what they needed, only to return home to their warm fires.

There seemed to be more night hours and the nights were darker. The skies were blankets of grey clouds which hid the light of the moon and stars. The wind even seemed eerie as it whined and moaned and sometimes reached the intensity of a shrill pitched sound that froze me in my tracks. In that silence, the wind entrapped me and filled me with foreboding. It was as if someone was speaking to me, yet, no one was there. Walking faster or running, I could not escape from it. Ever present, constant in sound, it moaned about me, following me home at night.

Arriving home, the wood steps creaked and the rusty screened door hinges rattled, announcing my arrival each night. The darkness inside was darker than the night outside. In total blindness, the house would engulf me.

Time and time again, I walked in loneliness and fear, and fled to the solitude of my small bedroom.

The tremendous exhaustion of my days allowed me to drift off into the safety of sleep. I would have my car coat hood drawn tightly around my head and tied under my chin. My hands would be in the pockets and my knees drawn up as much as possible underneath the coat.

It was late November and the temperature had dropped to 10 degrees below zero. The wind chill factor only made it worse. How I hated the wind. It blew and blew, and the whistling sound brought remembrances of the cold, hunger, and loneliness that traveled with me daily.

Shaking myself free of thoughts, I turned the outside lock on the drugstore door, and turned toward the street.

"Hey."

"Hey, Fay!" A car eased toward the curb. A man sat behind the wheel and a girl leaned across him to speak to me. I recognized her from high school last year. I thought she had graduated.

"Get in!" she yelled. "We'll take you home."

"Thanks, but I can walk," I said.

She replied with an emphatic, "No!"

"It's cold and Monte is working all night. And we are just going to be driving around," she said.

Yes, Monte was the local policeman, working night duty.

They were dating, and had nowhere to go in our small town with a population of 1103 people. I wondered if the three represented my brother and sisters who had been taken to Illinois. But chances were that we were not even counted in the census. I sometimes had the feeling that our family were like ghosts sitting on the perimeters of earth, and no one knew we were there.

I felt ashamed. I did not want to tell them that I lived out on the Project.

The $13.38 of take home pay, per week, covered the twenty dollars per month for rent plus the electricity, and the payment on the furniture I no longer had in my possession. But I did have a roof over my head, and a place to call home. And it left me a dollar a week for school lunches, and twenty cents per night for a dinner of two vegetables and a slice of bread at Lillie Mae Cole's, the little diner that sat next door to the drugstore. Additionally, I would accumulate a small amount of money to send to Mother for the kids. But, as I had listened from behind the soda fountain, I heard unpleasant references to the 'Project." I had enough to deal with without it being passed around at school that I lived out 'there.' Some had to know already. But I did not want to make it an issue.

They would not take a 'no' for an answer. There was no logical reason for me to refuse their offer, except my pride. I climbed into the back seat and told them I lived on the North Project.

The ride was short. "You can let me out here," I said at the corner of the Project.

"No, we will take you home. Where do you live?"

Again I hesitated. They insisted. I gave the directions: a right, a left, four blocks up, almost to the end and on the left.

The house sat, almost like a ghost, mostly dark with only a few distinguishable outlines.

I jumped from the car, thanking them, and waving goodbye, hoping to rush them on their way. But, even they were disturbed by the dark, ghostly, end of the earth, place. With the moaning wind, and starless moonless sky that blanketed the house's existence, they were hesitant about leaving me alone in the dark.

"We will wait for you to get inside before we go," Annette proclaimed. "So, we will know you are okay!" she shouted over the pitch of the wind.

They would not budge at my objections. I lingered slightly and slowly climbed the two steps to the tiny porch. I opened the door. They could not see me where I stood or hear the sound of the door opening above the whistling and moaning wind.

"Turn on the light," she yelled. "So we know you are safely inside."

I cringed. I didn't want to do it! But my numb fingers hit the light switch.

The light filled the empty front room, with neither curtains nor shades, and flowed into the darkness outside.

Waving again, I raced across the living room floor to my bedroom and hit the switch on the other side of the room. I stood in the darkness, against the door of my room, waiting for them to drive away. In the back of my mind I was hoping that I was alone in the house for another night. Safe for another day.

The afternoon school crowd had cleared out of the drugstore when Annette Hill showed herself for the second time. In an almost shy, and a polite manner, she asked, "Fay, do you live in that house by yourself?" It was so direct, but also unthreatening.

At that moment, no amount of pretense or excuses would work. The truth came simple and straight from my lips. "Yes."

"I talked with my parents when I got home last night," she was saying, "They know I have always wanted a sister, because, I am an only child. I asked them if you could come live with us. We have an extra room upstairs across from mine, and I have to sleep up there all by myself."

She was speaking fast. "And I only live two blocks from here. And it's between here and the high school. It wouldn't be near as much walking. You can stay free."

What a clincher!

She had said it all in one breath.

I stared at her, calling on all the resources of my knowing. She was being honest and did want me to come!

"Please think about it," she prompted. I told her I would. And I said to her that I would go to her house on Saturday. Saturday was a few days away. This delay would give me some time to think.

On Saturday afternoon we sat at the dining table in their sparkling clean kitchen. It had lots of black and white tile. They were on the wall, the counter top and on the floor. It looked like one became the other. We could have eaten off either. I had never seen a kitchen like that. I wanted to stare at it until my brain could accept this new picture in my mind as a 'kitchen.' This was the first time I had been in another family's residence except the shacks my relatives occupied. They were small and dirty. This house was large and airy. I felt comfortable in their home.

I had made some decisions. "I would like to stay with you. But, I won't eat off you," I told them. I still had my pride. I could only accept so much charity.

"That's okay," Mrs. Hill replied. And the matter was settled.

That evening, Monte, Annette, and I drove to the project. Monte went to my bedroom and loaded my small chest into the trunk of his car. I took my two changes of clothes off the wall and laid them in the back seat beside me.

Physically speaking, Annette's offer was a gift from the universe, but emotionally, I felt embarrassment and ashamed. It was all I could do to look them in the face for days.

I asked myself, "How many others would they tell?" Who else would now be 'looking down' on me and treating me more like an outcast?"

Being without family was one thing, but giving up my home and being homeless was another. It had been a very difficult decision.

But it did not take much common sense to see that I would be safer, warmer, and with less physical stress to my body, living closer to both school and work…no matter who knew that I no longer had a home.

I was reminded, again, of my first objective. I had to first survive and then finish my education. Nothing else even came close in importance. That included my pride.

I had to work on myself. But within days I was coasting along with my tunnel vision back. I had basically disassociated from my emotional feelings and need for social acceptance. I had to complete my aim and aspiration…survive, and get an education.

As a teenager I began to see a specific talent develop within me that was the most useful one I had discovered yet. Maybe it was all the hormones raging through my physically developing body, and all the sexual and emotional stuff that comes with it. My sexual needs, my social needs, my need for friends, family, love and intimacy, left my mind and body exhausted.

In order to maintain control over things, I separated out my emotional-self from my logical-self. I had actually started the process at twelve. Now, for most things, I could immediately discriminate between emotional inclinations or the logical, concrete decisions, and the action required.

Even if I allowed myself some reverie at times, I did so recognizing that my 'emotional-self' was a part of me, and it was as much under my control as that other part of me which I knew I must trust for my survival. And I could never let the emotional stuff get in the way.

My consciousness began to observe this process and found it easy to control the brain's functions. I had always been aware of my intuition, my gut feelings, and my body's innate ability to give me yes and no answers when trying to make decisions.

But the ability to separate myself into three different entities amused me! I knew this was all taking place in my head. However, this (1) 'awareness aspect' seemed to be 'me' and was somehow separate and superior to the (2) mind/brain or (3) my body. It was something inside of me, but also me.

Soon, I only followed its' guidance with true awareness that it was there. My tiredness, lack of sleep, physical pain, emotional and social pain or needs, could easily be set aside. And I would continue to function as expected of me.

While my voice was silent and my eyes steady, a continuous dialogue was taking place in my head. Every activity around me was being analyzed and pigeon-holed. It became a game of organization and structure...much more than just the activity itself. It was almost one of: I am one step ahead of you. It was somewhat of a survival tool, but more so, retaliation to some of the treatment I endured.

Whatever reaction I might have had to any situation was mentally compartmentalized before the comment was made, an attitude raised its ugly head, or I was obviously ignored or left out of a social interest. I looked, observed, anticipated, prepared, and as far as I was personally concerned, I was in control. The blows never hit me. The look or comment was unheard.

The brain had turned off the emotional impact before it happened. I simply switched from 'emotional brain' to 'logical brain'. My 'self' said, "You are doing great." I knew it was working for me.

Based upon the mental activities I had been engaging in, there exploded into my head again the profound realization that, "I am more than my body!" I had known it from birth. Why did I keep forgetting? The pull of society was causing me to forget the real me.

I had my physical body and my 'self' which was without form. And if my 'self' said so, the body responded accordingly. I could do and be anything I wanted to be, at any time. The body and brain were totally trainable.

As I retreated to the safety of residing within my 'Self' most of my days were like blurs on pages flipping by for the following months. I felt little and my days were nothing more than robotic movement through my waking hours. I did all that was required of me. There are few memories of work and school except the fact that I was there, occupied space, and passed the time. Somehow, society had not given me the right to ask for anything more.

# 33

## Pulled into the Social Group

1958

> *The beauty of it is, that no matter who you are, or who you are not, we are all on this path together, and we need the weak and the strong, the haves and the have-nots, to help along the way.*

The jukebox blasted Elvis Presley's Blue Suede Shoes. The after school crowd thinned out as the music seemed louder in the small Rexall drugstore with its pharmacy, cosmetic counter, and most importantly for Lilbourn High…the soda fountain.

Burr Middleton climbed upon the stool at the end of the fountain.

"Hi, Burr," I said.

"Hi, to you."

"What would you like?"

"I'm short this week," he said. "My last quarter just went into the juke box. How's my credit?"

They could talk to me all day, yell out their orders, say hello and goodbye, all to which I responded with a smile and a quick reply. But entering into a conversation with them was difficult. I was not a part of their world. I could not participate, not even in conversation.

My sweet silence offered him no condemnation or belittlement for the lack of funds on that particular day. I knew what it was like to have no money and how quickly friends ceased to be friends when you did not match their spending. And it also meant that to hang around the fountain, was having the resemblance of having the spending power for malt or a sundae even if you are not hungry. Penny candy would usually do. Two for a penny was even better!

"How about ten of these for a nickel?" Burr asks.

Mr. Jones had offered me his complete trust. I had given Burr credit before in similar amounts, knowing I would have to pay back his debt to Mr. Jones if Burr did not pay me, but he always did. Even though there had been only a few times.

"And five more of these."

Yes, it was early, and he would not have transportation home for a couple of hours, and he had to stall and feed the growls in his stomach for a while.

Burr was tall and thin, and rugged from hard and strenuous farm work. He was a basketball star. And he had been the 'steady' of Sue Neal for two years, who was a cheerleader and popular girl at Lilbourn High. But they had broken up.

He had some of the gentleness and respect that came from growing up on the land, trusting in God with each spring's planting, and never being boastful and arrogant. This comes from being aware that "as the earth giveth, the earth also taketh away," and the uncertainty of life makes one humble. This was something many of the town kids had not learned as they spent the constant flow of their parent's income.

He leaned forward with his clean-cut face and blonde crew-cut hair. His clear blue eyes were smiling at me. That moment of understanding and friendship passed between us. Whether it was an exchange on the soul level, or the moment of hesitation… which I will never know…he reached for the class ring on his hand and held it out to me.

"Keep this for collateral," he said.

My eyes glanced across the back bar of the fountain, wondering where I could safely leave the ring until he returned for it.

"No. Put it on the chain around your neck," he prompted.

"No," I replied softly. I knew what it meant to wear a boy's ring around my neck. It would be deceiving. We were not 'going steady!'

"Yes. You can put it inside your shirt. I will have some money Saturday…It's Tuesday…That's four days."

"Okay, until Saturday," I said.

Thursday afternoon the journalism class was lethargic from lunch and the traditional afternoon slump.

"Come on," Mrs. Thomas called, "the school paper comes out tomorrow. We've got to have some more stories!"

"I need some gossip for my column," Doris called.

"How about, Burr and Fay are going steady?" Burr said.

The whole class fell totally silent. He showed no evidence of kidding. He looked very serious, in fact. The class responded with various statements of, "Really!" "When?" "Is it true?"

Their eyes were now on me. Some with admiration, some with questioning. But to my greatest surprise, none with disbelief.

Was I really that acceptable to them? I had never been told that I was pretty. I had never had a date. And I only had three changes of clothing, which I rotated regularly. It couldn't be. My thoughts were stopped in mid-sentence by his next words.

"She has my ring around her neck."

They rushed to me as I gently pulled the ring from underneath my blouse, and placed it on top between my breasts. It felt warm, and good there.

Whatever his intention, I trusted him, and this was fun. Maybe with a little jealousy he could get Sue back, and in the meantime the small school of Lilbourn High would gossip indeed!

A week went by. I went to class as usual. I went to work

as usual. Whispers and glances wherever I went were a constant reminder of what it meant to be looked up to, to be a part of something I wasn't. I was not, and never had been a part of the dating world, and I was finding it difficult to extend the hoax.

The afternoon crowd had cleared out of the booths at the Drugstore. I was moving between the juke box and the booths, intent on cleaning the tables, when I was blocked by Sue Neal.

"You are not really going steady, are you?" she questioned.

"No. How did you know?" I could only answer truthfully.

"You don't seem proud enough."

Simply said, wisely observed.

Isn't it amazing how an incident will change our perception forever? My perception changed because of Burr's courage, or desperation. Whatever drove him to reach out to me, brought me closer to the realization that there is no "Me and Them" in this world. There is only "Us." All is one and the same! Since entering their world almost four years ago, I had come a long way in my understanding of things.

Nevertheless, I was still me. I was a survivor! Many times a survivor! And I looked at life differently.

At that point in my life, I had come close to dying of hunger and disease, had been physically and emotionally abandoned, and had risked my life by living alone.

I had reached the crossroad early in life knowing that I was not going to die, even if I felt like dying; which I often did. Dying would have been easy for me, many times, because life offered so little.

I knew existing on this earth had nothing to do with "deserving." You don't get more or less of what life dishes out because you deserve more or less.

If we place value on ourselves because of a belief that certain things have certain value, we cannot maintain a sense of worthiness. Because, conditions of life are not constant. Thus, how do we survive when we lose those physical things on which we have placed the value of our self worth?

I had nothing of monetary value. I had no family support to draw upon to promote my self respect, and no place or status within the community.

What I did have was an internal strength and courage to continue to face life day after day with dignity. I tolerated the difficult times with patience and sweetness. The good times I accepted with smiles and humility.

I was an observer of this strange phenomenon called life. But I chose not to be an emotional participant. In my world of experience, nothing was constant except the 'lack.' Lack of food, lack of clothing, lack of family, lack of friends, etc. There seemed to be nothing constant to tie me into other realities as a child or as a youth. There was nothing for me to become emotionally attached to.

When things went wrong, when others suffered loss, those around me became threatened, insecure, and lonely. By the age of eighteen I was already saying to myself, "Been there, done that!"

Burr was suffering from the loss of Sue, whom he had dated for two years. He was lonely. And he may have been, somehow, ostracized from the social group to which he and Sue belonged.

Because I was not emotionally tied into things, I did not judge Burr. My non-judgmental attitude toward him may have drawn him to me in his moment of need. Maybe spreading untrue gossip was an attempt by him to regain popularity and attention. Maybe (had it turned out that way) I could have become the laughing stock of Lilbourn High School, and he would have still been in the limelight.

I don't think it was his intent, originally, to use me. Neither could I believe that he could be interested in me as a girlfriend. It was another one of those times and happenings in my life for which there is no complete explanation. The beauty of it is that no matter who you are, or who you are not, we are all on this path together and we need the weak and the strong, the haves and the have-nots, to help the others along the way.

# 34

## Religion

1958

*Everything...in what could be called my spiritual experiences had been kind and loving, peaceful, and reassuring.*

Joy and Bill Jones belonged to the First Baptist Church of Lilbourn, Missouri. Each Sunday the store was closed between 10:00 am and 12:00 pm for church service. I was not familiar with the Baptist church. But, I did know something about another church.

I had met a classmate, Myrtle Watson, during the time that I was working on a part time basis at the drugstore. She was Pentecostal and went to the Assembly of God Church which was the same church my Grandmother and Grandfather had attended when I was ten years old.

When I began working full time, I needed to select a church to attend on Sunday. It was expected of me and I had nowhere else to go when the store closed. I decided to attend the Pentecostal church where Myrtle attended. There was another reason. I had also met another classmate, Patsy Fay Lawrence, who attended there. I felt a little more comfortable choosing that church because I knew some young people there and a little about the worship service, before I attended.

From the beginning, the worship service did not make sense to me. The loving stories of Jesus and his love I had heard in Sunday school at age ten was somehow reversed. The sermons were about how sinful we were and how wrathful god was going to be by putting us into a hellfire, brimstone, and eternal damnation. I sat through the sermons; shocked by each of them.

Everything…in what could be called my spiritual experiences was kind and loving, peaceful, and reassuring. I was not bad, wicked, and shameful.

The prayer time during the service seemed to go on and on. I listened as they begged, petitioned, and cried for mercy. Pleading for forgiveness for their sins was a common thread running through the prayers. I thought, "What is a sin? Doing something wrong? Am I doing something I shouldn't?" If I was, I couldn't figure out what it might be.

After each service was over I felt dirty, and my spirit was not as light as it had been when I came in.

After a few weeks I began to think about leaving. I would have to do so at the cost of losing contact with Myrtle and Patsy Fay. This was difficult because they were the first people in my life to treat me like a friend.

As I was pondering what I wanted to do, the decision was made for me. The 'church' had become aware and concerned because one of their members, (me) was engaged in the sinful activity of selling soda pop and cosmetics. The suggestion was that I leave such vile employment.

I left the church instead. Not that I had much choice since I could not survive by myself if I was not employed. But since I did not concur with their belief system, I was ready to leave the Pentecostal church.

I went to the Baptist church for the remaining time I was in Lilbourn. I never felt a part of the 'church family,' but I also did not feel so sad, guilty, shameful, and fearful. All I wanted and needed was to survive without something or someone holding me back.

The whole concept of religion, to me, became the church. It was an external thing, put together by adults with some very weird ideas. I could not see how all this behavioral stuff applied to me. It all seemed to be about behavior modification, and only showing one side of your behavior to the public. As I listened to small talk at the store, when no one thought I could hear or was listening, I began to see this church stuff as a game people were playing. I wasn't sure I would ever want to get personally involved in it.

I had already developed some concepts for myself about that energy source I drew from. Maybe it was the 'God' the church advocated. Maybe it was something else. I could not visualize them being one and the same. But I did not know what else it was either. Only that it was always there, and it never frightened me like the church.

# 35

## My Senior Year

Fall 1958 - Spring 1959

> *I just KNEW that in the greater realm of things, things were taking shape for my life.*

My rest of my senior year found me with the Hill family. Annette had found that I was not much of a sister. I had never related to anyone and really did not know how to be a part of the family. I came and went as school and work demanded.

After arriving at the Hill home, I learned that Mr. Hill was a mortician. There were three rooms upstairs. One was Annette's bedroom, one was my bedroom, and the third was a very large room filled with caskets. The door to the room with caskets was kept closed at night, but I never became comfortable climbing those stairs at night, or being alone upstairs. But I think that my presence in the room across the hall from Annette had some significance for her. Her parents never spoke of money, and were always kind.

Mrs. Hill worked outside the home. And Mr. Hill was always there because of the funeral business. He was about twenty years older than Mrs. Hill. That would have put them at about forty-eight and sixty-eight that year. He would come around me when she was not there. I tried to respect his age. But, I also tried to stay clear of him. I had good reason to trust no one. Everyone I had ever loved or trusted had hurt and/or abandoned me.

My plans were working out and I still had my tunnel vision for an education. I had written Southeast Missouri State University at Cape Girardeau Missouri, for information. It looked like I would have to save for a semester, go to college that term, stop and save for another semester, until I could get a better paying job or a scholarship.

It was during that time of saving for college that I came home one night from work and passed out in the bathroom. I had been living only on school lunches for weeks to meet my savings objective and was not getting enough nutrition. But it probably had as much to do with my psychological condition, as well. My mother had written me, asking for money for shoes and lunch money to keep the kids in school. I wanted to protect and provide for them as much as for myself. So, I sent her all my savings.

I was devastated. I knew at that point I would not be able to save enough money for my first semester tuition by the time the university term started in the fall. I was saddened by the thoughts of delaying my education.

I spent two weeks in bed before I could be up without blacking out. Dr. Chastain came to see me, even though I had no money to pay him.

Mr. Hill brought me some food for a couple of days and I felt better. He must have thought so too, because when he brought me food on the third day he sat down by the bed, and reached for my breast. I pushed his hands away. He persisted. I became very upset. My push was coming to blows. He backed away, glared at me, and accused me of being ungrateful. I did not touch the food he had brought and he did not come back to the room while I was there.

Mrs. Bell, my Home Economic teacher, lived across the street. She brought me a large bowl of fruit. I lived off the fruit for another week. Mrs. Bell never knew what that bowl of fruit meant to me.

Even without a lot to eat, the bed rest gave me back some strength, and I went back to work. Dr. Chastain had told Bill Jones, the owner of the drugstore, why I had been unable to work. Upon my return to work, Mr. Jones insisted that I fix myself a milkshake everyday, as soon as I got into the store from school, and not to worry about paying for them. I appreciated his willingness to help.

I tried that first week back in the store to drink the milkshakes, but my conscience and pride would not allow me to take food without paying for it.

I eventually paid for what I took, and chose instead, to spend the twenty cents cost of the milkshake at Lillie Mae Cole's diner next door for my usual vegetable plate of two vegetables and a slice of bread which I found more satisfying.

I did not send Mother any more money that year. It was almost spring time and I knew they could get some work.

And still uppermost in my mind was the fact that I had to survive. I was determined to do more than that. I did not know what or where. But I knew I had places to go, sights to see, and things to do with my life. I just KNEW that in the greater realm of things, conditions were taking shape for my life.

The spring of 1959 seemed to have more bustle and activities than our small community ever had. Maybe it was because it was my senior year at Lilbourn High. But more kids were getting automobiles, and Lilbourn boys were scouting out the New Madrid girls, and the New Madrid boys were over checking out the girls at Jones' Rexall Drugstore.

Some poor fellow was home from college for the Spring Break. Finding no favor in his home town (New Madrid), he ventured to Lilbourn. After sitting around the store playing the juke box and pinball machine all evening, he had not encountered one unattached female. That is, except me.

"Can I take you home?" he asked. It was more of a courtesy than a date request. He appeared almost as shy as I was.

"Yes, but I live close by," I told him.

"Well, maybe we can ride around a bit."

"Okay." (I had not spent that much time in an automobile! It was almost like an adventure.)

He waited until I had finished and escorted me to his car. The car wasn't bad!

He told me he was home from college and this was the first time his car had been driven in months. This was because as a 'work scholarship student' he was not allowed to have a car on campus.

"I'm looking for something like that," I said. "I plan to go to college, but I don't have the money for tuition."

"What about your family."

"My father is disabled. Mother is remarried and living in Illinois. I am living here working so I can go to school."

"Wow! This school is set up for kids like you," he said. "My father could have paid for me, but my parents think it is better if I work for my education myself. This college has a work scholarship program where you can work 540 hours in the summer for your year's tuition. Then you work 20 hours a week for your room and board when school starts."

"That would be great for me." I was excited about the prospects!

"There is a man in Popular Bluff who sponsors students from Southeast Missouri. He is sponsoring me. Would you like for me to give him your name?"

"Yes," I responded excitedly.

"He will send you an application. Just fill it out and send it back to him with a transcript. He will do the rest."

Within a month I had the application in hand.

I knew nothing of the school. But it seemed right! It was a perfect opportunity I could never have conceived.

It was interesting to me that no one at my high school or in the community ever asked me how I found, or rather, how the

College of the Ozarks found me.

It was customary for the school Principal to handle all transcripts. When I asked Mr. Taul to send them a transcript he neither questioned me about my plans nor agreed that he would do so. I assumed, at some point in time, I would know if he had or not. If not, I would have to ask for help from the school secretary or put pressure on him through Bill Jones.

There had been a string of things in my life that kept coming together following my wishes and desires for my life. Finding a possible work scholarship was one of many 'mini-miracle' that had happened in my life. My life was being filled with them. I waited expectantly for additional ones to happen. I fully trusted in the 'force' that surrounded and immersed me. I knew that my "God of the cotton field" had watched as I had done my part; and was now beginning to fulfill his end of the commitment we had pledged.

Come April, my letter arrived. It congratulated me on my acceptance to the college and its work program. I was to report to the women's dormitory on Monday, June 4$^{th}$, where I would be assigned a room and a work program. They looked forward to having me since they were set up to help indigent and worthy students, such as me.

# 36

## Moving On

*I had so far found the world to be mediocre, but I knew I was destined for so much more.*

And so my days at Lilbourn High School ended. No one in my family was there for the graduation ceremony. And I shrugged it off like everything else when it came to 'family.'

My time in high school had been mostly blurred days of mere existence. Nevertheless, those days served to establish and build inner strength and resolve. My high school days were also a strong validation to my strength and determination. There had been no ball games, parties, dates, and no moments to carry with me. There were few to say goodbye to. The space I had filled was replaced by another soda jerk at the drug store. I had been an observer of life, not a participant.

I had become an observer of life, because there was no place or way for me to fit in. My whole existence was totally out of step with all the other young people I came to know and observe from behind the counter and fountain.

A part of my survival was due to the fact that when my deeper emotional needs were pushed to the forefront, the rational mind projected itself outside my head, logically figured things out, and put everything neatly in its proper perspective. My feelings, needs, wants, and desires were stifled against the sheer will of my mind and soul that drove me and led me, and protected me from harm.

I would not and could not be satisfied, happy, or content, until I knew there could be a better life for me. There had to be some physical comfort, but just as important, there had to be a high degree of mental challenge, because my mind and my spirit could not be minimized. I had so far found the world to be mediocre, but I knew I was destined for much more.

## Chapter 37

## The Universe Sings

Saturday afternoon, June 2, 1959

*Within me I felt the love and reassurance of being worthy.*

High School Graduation had been uneventful. I did not have a good education, but I had graduated. A couple of people asked me about my plans. I simply replied that I would start college in the fall, but I would be leaving in a few days to where I would work for the summer on a work scholarship. I had the feeling that it was more than they wanted to know.

After four years of work in the store, in a small town, no one, including my teachers or principal, ever questioned my plans for college. They were busy getting everybody else ready. Maybe their lack of interest was because it appeared preposterous to any knowledgeable person who knew my circumstances. And it was unimportant to most, who without any personal interest had accepted the help and service of a shy, thin, unattractive, red-headed girl.

I could claim patience and sacrifice as virtues that brought me closer to my destiny, day by day. But since I had no one to be accountable to, I simply accepted my 'knowing.'

When a stranger walked into the store and sat on a stool at the fountain, I approached him smiling.

"Hello, you are new in town?"

"Yes, for just a day or two," he said.

"The same for me," I replied.

"Where are you going?" he asked.

"Branson, Missouri."

"That's where I live. What takes you to Branson?" he wanted to know.

"I'm due at the College of the Ozarks on Monday to begin a scholarship work program this summer for my fall tuition."

It was two days away, and I still did not know how I was going to get there. I 'knew' I would, I just did not know how.

"I don't know what plans you have made, (none, I thought) but I live just two miles from the college. I have a daughter your age. If you'd like to drive back with me tomorrow, you can spend the night with my daughter and we will take you to the college Monday morning."

"I am packed. That will be great! Thank you," I answered.

June 3, 1959

He chuckled softly to himself as his old station wagon climbed the hills and rounded the sharp curves, through the Ozark Mountains. Little did he know that the circumstances, flowing through his mind as he reflected on the past three days, had everything to do with the greater cosmic plan of the young freckled-face, red head girl that nodded sleepily at his side. The Universe had used his unfortunate situation to accommodate my need for transportation.

Waking from the few moments of relaxation, his chuckle had gotten my attention.

When I looked at him, he said, "I was just thinking. My wife and I have eleven children. I found her up in Alaska taking care of homeless children. We adopted them all. She is a wonderful person and doing her job far greater than I. We decided to come to Branson, where I had a job waiting for me. But when we got there, the job didn't work out. I have been walking the streets for weeks looking for work. I was down to my last dime, so I picked up the phone, deposited the dime, and called a minister friend of mine. I told him my situation and asked if he had anything I could do for work. The only thing he had, he told me, was that the church had a lot of clothing that needed transported two hundred miles to a Southeast Missouri Project, and it HAD to be done this weekend."

I smiled. Within me I felt the love and reassurance that comes from being worthy. I had never thought to question how I was going to get to the College, and now it all seemed so complicated…this great plan of managing and working things out for the good of all.

I could never have arranged this. I was glad to have someone else taking care of things for me…and College. I was ready!

# Epilogue

# Epilogue

I was traumatized by what I considered deprivation in five areas of my life: physical, emotional, educational, social, and religion. The traumatization that happened was because I constantly felt myself driven by the need for a greater purpose, knowledge, and wisdom.

I used the adage, "I do not know (what is available to me) what I want." I knew that I had to first rise above the conditions that I felt were depriving me of the essence of life. And until I could see what life had to offer me, I could only seek opportunities that I hoped would give me the life I wanted.

I did not understand at the time that my mind was counteracting the trauma of my life experiences in the mixed up ways I tried to survive. But I knew, alone, I could not have survived. As a result, I reached out to a force that I had only heard about. Being without form, it gave me not only strength and courage, but also wisdom.

In later years, I simply referred to it as my 'knowing.' I would say, "When I know that I know, that I know," then I would not question it. That 'knowing,' came from somewhere beyond me, without logic or information on the matter.

For years, I thought it was someone, or something, outside of me. Then, it gradually dawned on me that the creative intelligence was 'me.' It was my soul-self that was constantly in the driver's seat; driving me beyond the physical, the mental, the logical. It was a wonderful 'self' that transcended my body and mind. It was a beautiful and wonderful spirit that drew people, events, and situations into my life. It was a spirit that was constantly creating; creating things that I could not explain.

I, eventually, just quit trying to understand and explain the mini-miracles in my life. I simply accepted this precious life force, and the 'perfect lessons' it created for me.

I know now, beyond a doubt, that my soul, my spirit, my self, has a life of it's own to express, and this physical vehicle is going to enjoy every moment of the ride!

# Part III

# *Transformation*

# Chapter 1

## My Soul, My Spirit, My Self

*Interestingly, the most commonly taught lesson concerning Self is to control and deny, thereby conforming oneself to society or the desire of someone more powerful.*

It is not confusing to me that people find it difficult to define themselves today. In years past, the family and community defined who we were within their context. Since the 1950's, families have been diminishing as the nucleus of our western society. Technology has carried us from a 'local' to a 'world' community. Within the context of our global community, there are thousands of ways of defining ourselves. These 'self' definitions far surpass our family of origin, religion and community mores, certain political structures, and career choices.

As a result of this broader scope, our paths have become confusing, and we have lost the knowledge of the essence of who we are. Nevertheless, tremendous choices and opportunities are now presenting themselves for Soul, Spirit, Self, development.

If your world is looking a bit crazy at times, or maybe even extremely crazy most of the time, just remember that past experience has shown us that out of chaos will come a higher level of order that surpasses our previous level of existence. It covers both personal lives and societies.

With higher levels of scientific discoveries, better understanding and maintenance of the human body, and world communication technology, that which has been put last in the Western World (Soul, Spirit, Self), is now trying to be expressed and acceptable within mainstream thought. I am speaking of that one aspect of mankind which differentiates one individual from another and makes each person unique; the Soul within each of us.

These developments that allow more and also more rapid soul development, in the realms of spirit, mind, and psyche, are becoming generously available to us. That is, we have more avenues in which to express our selves and our creativity, and a wider range of audience.

I have always felt that the mind is the last frontier. New scientific discoveries may take us out into the Universe and make our lives easier but we do not evolve because we become more technically advanced. Growing an extra limb or other physical adaptation in not necessarily evolution. True evolution of mankind will happen through the evolution of our minds and the nature of our Spirit.

Advances in understanding the human Soul and Spirit are already developing as a major field of evolution in our society. And these developments are not happening by chance.

Advances always fall within the context of other factors. All these factors are often summed up as "timing." I am reminded of Jesus' Coming. His birth was perfect 'timing' for the political, social, and religious conditions of the world, at that time. The Roman Empire had spread across Asia Minor. After the chaos of war and upheaval, the country had settled down under the Roman Empire where roads had opened to all parts of the kingdom (the total world as they knew it), travel and commerce was open, a common language developed, law and order were established, and people were exhausted from trying to worship many Gods. With peace and prosperity at hand, the disciples of Jesus carried his teachings of monotheism throughout the land and it was acceptable to the people who wanted to simplify their lives and get on with a comfortable livelihood. Jesus' teachings were embraced by many (and probably somewhat misinterpreted), and the world was changed for the next two thousand years.

Scientific discoveries have rapidly changed our world in the past one hundred years. With the advances has come a gap between the scientific community and the rest of us. This means we use the telephone, the computer, the cellular phone, electricity, and the jet plane but we do not understand them.

Our acceptance of modern technology, while we do not understand them, indicates our arrival at a point in time where we can also accept that there is more to the human Soul, Spirit, Self than we understands. And our awareness of our own lack of knowledge and understanding about this part of our being, paves the way to our seeking a better understanding of our essence and of our Soul's essential nature.

The 'timing' is right for rapid development for mankind in the knowledge of Self awareness and Self consciousness. Mankind, around the globe, has been crying out for a greater understanding, and a grasping for purpose of this Life, which has been given to us. Is it precious, or dispensable? Are there absolutes or total free will? Is this all there is? Is there more after we make our transition to the spiritual realm, if, indeed, there is a spiritual realm? How do we exist with such uncertainty?

Most don't! They grasp on to something. It may not be complete. But it is better than nothing at all. They hold on to whatever they have and search for the rest. It is this searching that is forming the chasm into which our mindset is falling. And it is out of this chasm that I think a new understanding is coming. From chaos to order, a new order where 'man' is the focus, equal to, if not instead of, science and technology.

The East needs another twenty years to completely put Western technology into place. In offering technology for capitalist purposes, the West will have greater exposure to Eastern Philosophy, which is permeating medicine even today, for the second time in 2000 years (Jesus studied there before his ministry). I pray that peace and prosperity in the world today will again nurture the spiritual aspects of man's essence in the West. And the 'timing' will be right for a new depth of knowledge concerning man's awareness of Soul-Spirit-Self.

Does that mean there are no answers now? The big answer is, 'no.' There are answers and solutions to our dilemma. Research, technology, and communications will bring us to a wider, deeper, more extended understanding of what it means to incarnate on this earth plane. But, I dare say, we will each find it necessary to find our own 'acceptable' philosophy.

Does this not leave us in the same situation we are in now? The answer is no! There may never be absolutes but, it will not be the same. We will have a wider range of choices for solution. I speak of solution for healing of the ecology, society, and the body. I speak of healing that starts with the individual and spreads to the masses. This type of transition starts as a subculture and is incorporated into the larger culture. It goes from micro to macro. It also moves in both directions. I think this new emphasis will be different, with focus on life forms of all kinds. Preserving, nurturing, accepting and respecting any and all life forms from around the globe, and maybe throughout the universe, as sacred and free to follow 'soul' while sharing our essence with one another.

I wish I could envision a utopia. How nice that would be. But to live in a perfect society, would also mean being born with perfect inclinations to meet the norms of whatever society we are born into. There is a field of thought that says, "The entire world is perfect." If we could all believe that the universe and all within it are perfect creations of a god-force, there would be no word in our vocabulary to indicate 'problem,' 'wrong,' 'little-big,' etc. There would only be 'I am,' 'it is,' without further definition. The development of our language has created differences, degrees, contrasts, and a perceived need to judge. If we could eliminate being judgmental of one another, we would indeed have to conclude that without judgment, we are perfect!

Could man go from where we are, to a place in the heart that accepts all behavior with respect?

The Behaviorist advocates that all behavior is caused. And our court system seeks to assign punishment based upon reasonable cause. At some point the behavior or action is acceptable. To another degree it is punishable.

The Learning Theorist says all behavior is learned. Therefore, anything done outside norms is punishable to promote reform of behavior.

But the question that remains open is: "Where is the Soul in the situation?"

Hitherto, the Soul has been neglected or totally ignored. If mankind considered itself spiritual beings, (a lot of religious institutions say so) how can it ignore the soul/spirit/self amid our highly legalized system of judgment? Has our lack of interest in the human soul allowed us to come too far in the wrong direction? Why have we not developed something better to offer those who step outside the boundaries of a society?

We have such limited, acceptable information, spiritually speaking. Therefore, we have no concrete basis for 'accepting' and 'nurturing' the activities of the Soul.

The greater part of our criminal population is incarcerated in our prison system at some time. Only a small part is rehabilitated to any worthwhile degree. (That degree amounts to staying out of trouble with the 'Law.') That is not to say that there has not been great effort in a great many ways, by a great many experts. But without a body of acceptable evidence concerning our spiritual needs (soul), how can we counsel?

Let us differentiate the practice of a religion here from spiritual knowledge and the use of that knowledge to counsel, help and correct behavior. Spiritual healers are not commissioned to teach a gospel or specific code of conduct. Their interest and power is to understand 'soul' and its path, and to communicate for understanding and wisdom. Religion, on the other hand, tends to judge, simply by its own nature. People who are out of control do not need judgment. They need wisdom and access to a different perspective.

Most people will never find themselves behind prison bars or the recipient of more than an occasional traffic ticket. (I speak mostly of traffic tickets in the United States. This is not as common in other countries, since most countries do not use traffic ticket fines as a means of generating income for local governments.)

So, we have some form of stealing, cheating, and lying, as the actions for crimes against others. And the basis for these is more often selfishness for our own sake. Most crimes can be interpreted as 'I want,' which results in harm against another. The original intent was not for the sheer joy of hurting another. (Although, there are the criminally insane (sociopath) and those whose personal pain is so great that their motive is to hurt or get even.)

So, the Self is saying, "I am not satisfied." Meaning, I want, I need something more. Behavior patterns become erratic, spontaneous, using whatever situation that lends itself for the Soul's expressed need. The Soul will take advantage of any opportunity. It will take from others to satisfy 'Self.'

Interestingly, the most commonly taught lesson concerning Self is to control and deny, thereby conforming oneself to society or the desire of someone more powerful. Therefore, the source of fulfillment is through the gaining of power and its perceived uses.

If enough power is not given to us or given soon enough for our desired Self development, it is likely to result in our taking power and control over situations and others to satisfy that need.

Our needs come in many forms and degrees. How different the results would be if as children we were taught to ask for, and received, those things, which we needed to be soulful individuals. At the same time being taught, and understanding that all needs are acceptable within some context, (and with the understanding for us as adults that that context will differ from society to society). Again, timing is a key factor, beginning in childhood. Saturation of Self is not good, nor is giving up 'Self' acceptable. Only proper sequencing and timing can give satisfactory results. And at this point in our cultural and religious process, the right sequencing is only by chance.

## Deprivation Trauma

The soul-self will actualize itself through any avenue available to it without concern for wrong or right. It will simply create experiences to express the self's most perfect lesson during our corporeal life. The lesson fits the soul's need, not that of a society. In a society where the social and political order is based upon a religion or a restrictive government, the soul stands to suffer. This is because there can be no personal or social expression of the soul outside the boundaries of that philosophy.

So, what will help lead the way among all the obstacles? Individual progress can lead the way. And it is happening at this moment. If you feel separated, disconnected, and/or your life hasn't been going like you would like, you can begin today by raising your level of consciousness and coming to understand that you have within you an innate intelligence that has the 'vision of God' concerning your life. And you can tap into it. Your innate intelligence will guide and direct your life in a way that will lead you to your greatest good. Its deeper knowing can answer questions from the mind. It can heal and restore your body. It works on a cellular level and is constantly trying to communicate. It will provide a path to express what you came to earth to experience, within the confines of society.

## Chapter 2

## The Process of Healing

> *How your mind responds to or interprets the experience determines your health.*

Speaking outside the realm of miracles, which happen in brief moments of prayer or peak experiences, we gain insight and growth on a continual basis. Sometimes it comes in large doses, and sometimes in small doses. I say 'doses' because we take in life like medicine. Some of life's experiences are just so-so, some are sweet, and some experiences 'do not taste too good.' The bitter and sweet experiences may affect us in profound ways. *This is because our mental response to the outside world determines our dis-ease with our physical experiences, and is reflected within our body. This is what is called mind-body connection. When something happens to your body; how your mind responds to or interprets the experience determines your health.*

Let us take some examples. Years ago, it became evident that people who were 'stressed out' showed up at doctors offices complaining of chronic ailments. These ailments included: headaches, stomach and/or digestive problems (acid reflux, heartburn, bloating, diarrhea, and constipation), fuzzy minds, back and neck problems, sleeping disorders, eating disorders, depression, joint problems, chronic fatigue, panic disorders, and any number of other aches and pains.

Stress is the body's negative response to an unfavorable situation or series of events. Many stressors are work, marriage, children, education, and can be any type of social relationships and activities. This can includes anything or everything around us! Our degree of mental and physical health is determined by how we mentally react to and handle this outside input. Therefore, our lives are lived in good health or our bodies can become stressed because we are not 'aware' and exercising control over how our bodies are responding to our environment.

The whole process of transcendence is to pull together your inner strength and personal power to create new things in your life. But in doing so, we must understand that life is like a training camp. Everything here is to teach us something and to promote growth. Whether it brings us pain or pleasure, the concept we want to remember is, 'What is life teaching us?' Sometimes it is, 'What is life showing us?' From the answers to these two questions we gain the wisdom to make wise choices. It does not seem to matter if the things that happen in our lives are considered good or bad. That is only a perception. Eventually, we come to realize that the changes we are sometimes forced to make are for our good. Sometimes we even look back and think that the worse times were are best times because of the differences they make in our lives.

So, if you are looking for ideas to bring you to a more conscious and healthier life (transcendence), try some of the ideas listed below. They worked for me!

## *Step 1*
## *- Life is a process.*

The first step in my transformation and healing process was to grasp the idea that life is a process. It happens from conception to the day we die. And it doesn't matter when we decide to make changes in our life, but that we make a 'commitment' to do so. And we may need to make commitments at different times in our lives to deal with different problems that arise. Rarely, can we say, "I am healed/unstressed," and remain 'healed/healthy' for the rest of our life. Something new always comes along to teach and to strengthen us.

The transformation, as a result of each experience, actually takes place when we have learned the 'perfect lesson,' which life is trying to teach us. When we have that 'aha' moment, the chances are that we will not have that same experience again. This is because we have (finally) learned that lesson. And our body and mind releases the tension and stress associated with this experience. After the release we may also find that this particular thing in our life does not carry any importance to us.

Now we can go on to the next, and the next experience. That is what 'life' is; a series of experiences that deepen our understanding of what it means to be hu(God)-man. All life is good, from the proper perspective. Even the most difficult experiences can teach and strengthen. But, we must open our minds (consciousness) to the experience. If we do not learn from the experience, a similar experience will most likely come around at another time. So keep moving forward, noting each and every experience and asking what life is showing you.

When our lives seemed unburdened; that is the time we should be available to help others who need help, compassion, or understanding. If we are finding that we do not find the time and resources to be of much help to others it is because of our own neediness demanding our time and resources. Don't beat yourself up over this. Just acknowledge it and commit to broadening the scope of your life.

The most important thing to remember is that when things are bad or not going well, don't get stuck! Open yourself to the experience. Ask, "How can I grow through this?" "Is there another way of looking at this situation?" Become aware of your emotional response to everything happening. Let go of anger, resentment, and fear. Forgive everything and everybody. Don't get stressed out! Let it go! The circumstances may or may not improve, but your health will not suffer because of it!

## Step 2
### - Healing is an inside job.

Number two in the transformation process is to know that healing is an inside job. Our body's emotional response to the outside world will determine our physical health and perspective on life. ***We must accept events without negative emotional reactions, and use our rationalization skills to survive while we consider our choices.***

I truly believe that we were given 'free will' by the grace of God, so we can co-create with God those things in our lives that we need. Make it a mindset to ***never, never, say that you do not have choices!*** If you remember Fay's situation, she realized that she had choices, but for most of her life they were all choices between two bad situations. But, she kept making choices instead of defaulting to someone else's choice. In other words, she was aware that she had only bad choices and chose (her choice) to wait. She chose to wait until better choices became available to her. When they did come, she moved forward. Some choices are like that. Some are get out, NOW!

It is important for our lives to honor the Universe (what comes our way). To honor Life and the Universe we must accept the things that confront us daily. To do this we can not leave ourselves emotionally depleted by yielding to an emotional roller coaster ride. These ups and downs and highs and lows take away our energy and leave us emotionally exhausted. We must police our responses and maintain our peace.

Another drain on our energy is holding on to too many people and situations. It is important that we let go of things that we tend to dwell upon if they are negative. It can sometimes become a waste of our creative energy. Our emotional energies can pull us down if they are negative. On the other hand, our positive emotional energies are the ones we use to create. Holding on to negative people and situations only slows us down.

There is a negative side to many things. So I must mention that 'letting-go' can be a conditioned reflex. As such, it can serve us well as long as we do not over use it as an escape mechanism, where nothing in life matters; therefore we have nothing serious to deal with. A similar escape mechanism that is unhealthy is blaming the universe for our perceived failures or transferring individual failures to others around us.

Everything in our life begins with our personal response. The object is not to stop the response, but to make it a consistently positive, healthy response that leaves us our energies to create positive things in our life.

## *Step 3*
## *- Leave the disfunctioning part of yourself/life behind.*

Transformation Process number three is to understand that to heal, we must leave the disfunctioning part(s) of ourselves and possibly other people in our lives, behind. We must turn away from bad habits, conditions, and sometimes other people in our lives.

We each grow at a different pace. When it is our time to grow, to give up an addiction, or make changes, it may mean losing friends. To walk away from an abusive relationship may create hardships for us and others. Remember, you cannot afford feelings of guilt and shame when it is a matter of life and death.

When your consciousness tells you something in your life is not right for you, it is time to seek wisdom and to give your life a new sense of direction. This step leads to the fourth step.

### Step 4
### *- Unload, sort out, and get a grip on things.*

The fourth step states that somewhere in the process we will need to 'unload,' sort out, get a grip on things, and see where we are in the process. This could mean writing in a journal, talking to a confidant, or seeking professional help. When we are highly conscious of things, we still need to get them outside our head. It is hard to get a sense of direction when the information keeps going around in a circle. So, get out of the mental loop and communicate it in linear form. We can gain more insight by viewing things from outside of ourselves.

### Step 5
### *- We are controlled by our beliefs.*

The fifth step is to know and to understand that we are controlled by our attitudes, beliefs, and behavior patterns.

Every government desires to totally acculturate the populace of that country. (Just think of all the help and tax concessions the U.S. government and other countries give to religion.) By doing so, they are able to control behavior. Our deep sense of right and wrong, good and bad, acceptable and unacceptable may have more to do with our daily life than we have ever imagined. The beliefs, attitudes, habits, and expectations of family, friends, church, schools, and government may override any desires we may have for our growth and even safety. But how are we able to grow and reclaim ourselves at the expense of losing our family, friends, and community? We must move on to number six.

## Step 6
### - Take care of yourself, before you try to care for others.

Step six, is taking care of you first. If we do not take care of ourselves; then we cannot take care of others. That goes beyond the simple person of you. It includes the true you, your Self; that Spiritual being on this physical journey. No one is truly responsible for us, except us. We are responsible for our body, our mind, and our spirit. To take care of the body we must give it a safe environment, proper food, rest, exercise, and get rid of bad habits and addictions. For the mind we must have peace, love, and validation as the unique person we are with individual needs, desires, and opportunities. We must be able to express our creativity. This is how the mind experiences our God Source.

Creativity is evidence of the Spirit within. If you wanted to be an artist, but ended up being a mother with four children, you can still be an artist. Your everyday activities provide innumerable opportunities. Instead of just baking a cake, decorate it with all the unlimited ideas, and resources available to you! Arrange your furniture as if you are composing a great work of art. Or do a sculpture for a fundraiser.

If you are a father who took an eight to five job, a "good job," to support your family when you really wanted to make it in the music industry, then, sing/play for your family, church, company activities, or do a fundraiser. Further, still, organize a block party in your neighborhood and entertain your neighbors!

The objective is to find creative ways to create, and to express Soul (innate talent). Find ways to do whatever the real you 'needs' to do. Hopefully, it can be done within your present situation. Otherwise, you will need to consider other solutions. In any case, do not be fearful of considering the decisions/choices available to you or the ones that you will need to create.

## *Step 7*
## *– Set reasonable goals.*

Goal setting is an exercise in finding a way of getting from here to there. When we begin and where we begin is not important. What is important is that we make a choice to begin and actually start the process. If we decide to do nothing, be aware that that is a choice, and we are making a decision to do nothing. And in some cases that decision could kill or harm someone.

Setting goals is important because it creates a road map to where we want to go. Only we can decide the best way for us to get there, and how slow or fast we will travel. One word of caution; be gentle on yourself. If you are trying to be conscious of what is happening in your life and you miss something, and it comes around again, don't beat yourself up over it. If it comes around again, this would generally be considered 'good'-- a second chance. Ask yourself questions (What happened? How did I miss it? What should I look for next time? Etc.), make mental notes for future reference, and move on.

*This book is about raising your level of consciousness to become more aware of what is happening in your life and how you can control your health and create wholeness in all things.* The chances are that we do not become fully conscious and an enlightened being overnight. But, we can get there by identifying and implementing small changes in our lives that can be controlled.

Our goal may be to control our emotional reactions to a given person or a given situation, to get off the pity-wagon, stop a bad habit, show more kindness, control our finances, change jobs, go back to school, treat a wound (emotional or physical), etc. We must decide how much change we can handle at one time so that we do not become discouraged in the process.

Whatever the goal, we must decide how we are going to go about the task. What will we do? What tools will we use? What are the mile markers? Who will help us, who will hinder us, and who will not matter either way?

A simple beginning, before we tackle larger problems of life, is to watch our emotional response to everyday situation. Start working on getting rid of negative emotional responses. Read books to increase knowledge and understanding of consciousness. And most importantly, create an attitude that life is something that we control and not something that happens TO us. Develop an attitude that says we have choices in our emotional reactions to all things, and can also choose to act at the moment or postpone action and/or decisions to act until things are more in our favor. We have personal power. We are in control.

## Step 8
### – Open yourself to life's experiences.

Life is a gift of experiences to be enjoyed. But experiences also teach. If within these experiences we practice being aware of our surroundings and what is happening and being said, we can increase our level of consciousness. We can then begin the process of consciously creating.

By consciously creating we create our own reality. We can change negative thought patterns. We can change our emotional responses to outside events/activities. We can come to recognize our myriad attitudes and belief systems, how our buttons gets pushed, and how our attitudes and belief systems propel us forward or hold us back. We can come to understand how our behaviors and responses affect others. We can become more in touch with our feelings and can prevent that emotional roller coaster ride we often experience. We may find that there are things about ourselves and our life that we do not like and want to change. We may find that we are really a great person, worthy of love and respect and need to stop being so hard on ourselves. We may even come to know who we really are and create the experiences that will bring us good health, joy, and happiness.

## Step 9
### - Develop awareness.

Even when we open ourselves to life's experiences and learn to look upon them as a gift to be enjoyed and from which we may learn, we may forget that we also have a task. The task can become cumbersome or exciting depending upon our attitude. The task of being always 'present' mentally wherever we are and whatever we are doing is a big responsibility. It should be a task that we take on gladly. Because the return on our investments are great.

To begin developing our inner awareness, the first things we may notice is what is called, 'self-talk.' There may be a continuous dialogue going on in our head. And unless we have it under control, it is probably making negative statements. We may develop this rationale early in life while we are trying to learn what is expected of us from parents, teacher, religious leaders, and others. It begins to pop up to remind us that we have forgotten something, or may have done something wrong. It might say something like, "You stupid idiot. You did it wrong again." "Why can't you do anything right?" "You forgot again." These may be words said to us by others and we repeat them to ourselves. And the words become a habitual repetition in our head each time we slip up or make a mistake. This negative self-talk lowers our opinion of ourselves, and can lead to feelings of unworthiness. We will want to catch them and turn them around to a positive statement. We might respond to these comments by saying, "I do many things right." "I have a high degree of intelligence." "I remember most things." "I rarely make mistakes." By doing so we are developing a consciously healthy attitude and belief system about ourselves, and we will continue the corrections until the negative comments are erased.

Our awareness can expand to the observation of others and their belief systems, attitudes and/or behavior patterns. As an experiment, pick a person near you either physically or emotionally. Ask, "How do they treat me?" "How do they respond to me?" "Do they treat me with disrespect?" "Apathy?" (i.e. Your behavior really does not matter to them.) "Do they put me on extensions?" That is, do they refuse to interact with me as a punishment because my behavior is not pleasing to them, and they want to let me know it? What does this information tell you about others?

Now that you are aware of their behavior can you translate it into their attitudes and belief systems? (i.e. Maybe the person is a man who has little respect for women. Maybe the person has more money, more education, a better job, etc, than you, and because of their ego, has chosen not to include you in their life.) These things reflect their value system and foster their attitudes. It is neither good nor bad. What is good or bad is your response.

Do either you or another respond with anger or hostility because both of you are doing things or saying things to the other and making demands that is contrary to a sense of well being? On this point, you must be specific. What game are you playing? What emotional response is generated between you and the other person? Is this emotion being generated as a means to gain control over you, or the other person? You may find that gaining or giving up control is a primary factor in much of your interactions. This is not healthy.

Now find a person whom you feel is supportive of you, and interacts with you, on an equal basis. This is a healthy relationship because they are not trying to take away your personal power. Think of ways this person validates you, supports your strengths, doesn't 'put you down' when you make a wrong decision or a mistake, recognizes your need to be human and stands by you in your hours of sadness, grief, disappointment and loss.

And just as important, recognize how many lives in which YOU play this respectful and supportive roll. Does hurt and fear prevent you from being strong and supportive for others?

Open yourself to honest appraisal. Do you want to live more consciously? This is a cognitive process. If so, you must develop an awareness of the real you and your thought processes and emotional reactions. Make a list of your attitudes and belief systems and where they came from. (moral issues, behaviors, customs, values)

You are what you think. Do you think you are separated

from a God Source, or whatever name you refer to the Universe outside the body? Can you search within and find your Soul, your true Self that can lead and direct you on this journey of life? If you can, the Soul is our connection to higher/greater realms of information and understanding and will take the difficulty out of our path. If you think you are only your 'personality/ego' self, then you have indeed separated your true Self from the Source of transpersonal experiences and expressions. But you can still make positive changes in your life by developing your awareness of your relationship with others and creating positive thought processes to strengthen your self-esteem and come to recognize your learned attitudes and habits.

### *Step 10*
### *- 'Coping Skills,' 'Survival Skills,' and 'Defense Mechanisms' are not dirty words.*

Sometimes we just need to survive for the time being. It can be a long journey to becoming safe, and/or emotionally and physically healthy. Being 'aware' is the first task at hand. The next is 'coping' with life and its difficulties. We must have tools and resources to maintain ourselves while we 'grow.'

To cope, at times, you may be the only person to tell yourself how great a person you are, to recognize your many talents, and to recognize the strength you have that has made you successful or a survivor. Your survival skills may be your awareness and permission to stay away from a person (or persons) that hurt you, bending the rules for your own benefit, relying on a God Source outside yourself for strength and hope.

Defense Mechanisms can be learning new communication skills to redefine relationships, finding your own voice to speak up on your own behalf, and staying away from the hand that would hurt you.

There are many defense mechanisms that apply to different situations. And if you need to defend yourself, cope for the time being, and survive a particular situation, you should draw on your personal power to protect yourself.

To change or correct a personal and/or business relationship, or protect your life and well-being, your personal power is expressed by your use of the skills you use to defend and promote yourself. If you are able to defend and promote yourself well others will say of you, "He/she is a 'strong' person." They recognize and respect your 'strength of person.'

Personal power is a must. It is sustained by the tools we use to live and to create. The need and use of tools is not a weakness because the tools allow us to maneuver around barriers we find in our way. Without the tools we would be less efficient in life and may even be blocked from achieving our goals.

Your coping skills can make or break you in life. This means you need them all of your life during the good times and the bad. We have already talked about the difficult times and examples of their use in these situations. The 'good time' coping skills help you deal with difficult people, situations, and even uncomfortable times in your life through out the year.

Your coping skills, survival skills, and defense mechanisms allow you to stand up and fight when you can safely do so, or use your rational to keep yourself safe when necessary, and allows you the fortitude to say, "I believe in myself and my right to have a healthy, happy, productive life of my own choosing."

## Step 11
### - Forgiveness.

I have said it before. Now, I am saying it again. The lack of forgiveness will hold you back! Who do you forgive? What do you forgive? The answer is; everybody and everything. I have a favorite saying; 'let go and let God' (take care of the situation). One of the greatest gifts I will ever receive came from my brother as I was standing by his grave after the funeral. He said, "Sis, don't sweat the small stuff." He meant for me to stop exerting so much of my energy on things that were not really important in my life. I had to let go of small stuff and find only the things that were important in my life and allow them to occupy my attention. I had to forgive and forget a great deal of 'stuff.'

Somehow, within life's process, we are taught to judge first, before all else. So, we judge, then we criticize, condemn, and censure. And in the long run, what we are doing is judging others by our own behavior and social expectations. In return, we judge ourselves by the same judgment we give others. In our judging we are reflecting ourselves outward.

To get rid of our anxiety, guilt, and fear of judgment from others, we must give up judging ourselves and forgive ourselves first. Then when we accept the forgiveness for our own mistakes, failures, and pain, and no longer have to carry that burden, we can then forgive others.

You may be thinking, "I can never forgive that person." If it was easy there would not be so many people hurting today. Yes, your un-forgiveness is actually hurting you!

I used to say that hating and not forgiving my mother was my favorite sin. (Separating me from my God-source.) But within a higher realm of consciousness, I knew that it was me that was hurting most. I had to release that pain. When I forgave her, my body actually released the trauma associated with her, and the bad memories were released from my mind with the emotional impact they carried. I realized that my sense of joy and peace had been denied me for years because I had been holding on to that anger, pain, and un-forgiveness.

An exercise to test how judgmental you are is to go for an entire day without forming an opinion (about right, wrong, good, bad). Don't judge anybody or anything. You can go back to yelling at the traffic and politicians tomorrow. Just for today, when you respond with anger, fear, anxiety, remorse, grief, hatred, ask yourself where that emotion is coming from. What belief system do you have that prompted that particular reaction? At the base, you have most likely been making a judgment. Let us take a simple example of what happens in life. Pick a belief you have about yourself or something else. If you can figure out why you accepted and held on to that belief, you are on your way to understanding your judgmental nature. That is not to say that your beliefs are wrong or incorrect. You must question why you feel threatened and feel a need to correct others who wish to live their lives differently. Then if you can eliminate the desire to correct the world to your self-imposed standards you will, yourself, have more freedom to make choices. If you listened instead of judging, there might be a perspective you had not considered.

Gently remind yourself that you desire a positive attitude towards things in your life. (This is a choice.) In this case, positive reactions are preferable to negative reactions which bring about the need to judge and correct, and that also brings about dis-ease in your body. Or if you are on the receiving end of someone's judgmental nature don't allow yourself the anger, fear, anxiety and grief of that relationship. It may take years from your life.

Forgiveness is a form of letting-go emotionally of people, things, and situations. Combining the words forgive and forget may take on a deeper meaning when you consider that only when you can 'let-go' and forget about something can you forgive. In fact, that is exactly what you are doing! You are forgiving! The simple exercise of holding something in your mind and dwelling on it is not forgiving. So, forget it. Move on.

# Pass Me By

*Time is a continuum of man's devise,*
*following the illusion of circumspect,*
*that fulfills the denial of soul and the eternal.*

*When does the state of being find meaning?*
*Surely not when things of past and future contrive*
*to define what is today.*
*To be bound by any manifestation other than*
*this precious moment prevents change, growth,*
*and freedom. Most of all, freedom!*
*To take away my today by judging it as*
*anything else is prison indeed.*

*Do not bring me your fear, guilt, shame, or*
*your judgment, worse of all.*
*I choose to not give up my joy, my peace,*
*to squander in the hell of your condemnation.*

*Accept today as today—if you must label life so.*
*Meet me in unconditional love as our journeys*
*pass. And I, too, release you unto your destiny.*

## Step 12
### – Make 'Transpersonal' a word in your vocabulary.

You are more than a body. You are a body, a mind, and a soul. The body is a vehicle for the Soul. The mind, in a sense, is a vehicle for the Soul to reach out to the Infinite Mind. To do so, one must go beyond personal identity; ego/personality, and duality which separate us from a higher source.

The evolution of living consciously causes the idea of separateness to dissolve. There is no longer a separation between the internal and external world when we reach an at-one-ment with our mind and our Source. (In the Bible the at-one-ment is the same as to atone for our sins. In other words, when we atone we are not separated from God.) One transcends co-dependency on people, places, things, events, and time. One's reality changes as the illusions fade.

There is an internal approach to knowledge and wisdom through the transpersonal approach to healing. When we become mindful (conscious) of our innate abilities and patterns in our thoughts and behavior, we change the pattern to be open to what 'Soul' wants to express through our being. Our lives become a pursuit of our innate talents, desires, and a quest for joyful living. We appreciate that life is a gift to be enjoyed and not suffered.

Listening within allows one's innate wisdom to inform and guide like an audio tour. More than likely it is telling you something you would rather not hear, rather than you listening and not hearing anything. So keep the channel open and seriously consider anything that comes into your mind.

Via the higher mode of consciousness, the transpersonal self leads to an inner-connectedness with the God-source and we become individual expressions of the Universal Mind/Divine Intelligence as co-creators for the evolution of mankind.

The transpersonal approach to healing keeps you from reactive thoughts that influence your health, and fosters a peace that is independent of the conditions around you. This is the bottom line.

Everything else is what takes you there.

# Light Came A'Creeping

*Light came a' creeping and man's eyes*
*Fluttered. Easier to think of tranquility and sleep*
*than knowledge.*
*Knowledge did not remove the toil.*
*Wisdom was little use in the mere struggle*
*of man with nature.*

*Light came…a'creeping.*
*Man's eyes fluttered.*
*A beam absorbed was a century in*
*the taking.*
*Man's struggle with man, found no grace*
*in illumination.*

*Light came…a…creeping. The Universe*
*whispered, "Why does man sleep?"*
*Nature answered, "I am more present."*
*"I fill his body and soul.*
*Those who seek find only confusion. And find*
*only closed ears amid others' denial."*

*Light…came…a…creeping. Many were awake!*
*The soothing pleasures of Nature could not ease*
*the seeking of the restless Souls.*
*Light surrounded and breathed in, and passed on*
*with healing joy.*
*Man becomes "one" with the light.*

~ Zalora Price ~

# Appendix 1 - Worksheet

Areas of deprivation in life with possible traumatic results.

| Physical | Emotional | Social | Educational | Spiritual | Other |
|----------|-----------|--------|-------------|-----------|-------|
|          |           |        |             |           |       |

# Acknowledgements

The persons in my life helped put the words on the pages of this book. They chose their parts, and played their roles. Some names have been changed at my own discretion.

Putting the book together was another story. For the love, encouragement, and patience, I want to thank my husband of forty + years, William J. Price. My children, Bryant Price and Ben Price stepped up to help when needed. Their computer and graphic skills are the best money can buy. My heartfelt, "Thanks," to both of them. And, a very special, 'thank you,' to my friends, Dennis Tardán and Melissa Roth-Tardan, for reading Deprivation (Part 3) and giving me a thumbs-up. Ben Price, Lia Price and Copper Welch also read the manuscript and made recommendations. Their comments were appreciated.

## About the Author

Zalora F. Price graduated from Drury University, Springfield, Missouri with a BA Degree in Psychology and Sociology. She became certified to Teach English through the University of Maryland, Townsend, Maryland. She is a Reiki Master Teacher, Certified Body Talk Practitioner, Spiritual Counselor, and Author. She has lived and traveled extensively through out the world. She maintains a home in Victoria, Texas to be near her two married sons.

## Copies of this book may be ordered from:

Laurel Publications
6029 Country Club Drive
Victoria, Texas  77904
Phone: 361-573-7254
Fax: 361-572-3894
Web sites:
www.DeprivationTrauma.com
www.ZaloraPrice.com

Please include check or money order for $16.95 (USD) plus $4.00 for postage and handling. Texas residents must also include 8.25% ($1.40) for state sales tax.

Web site customers can use Visa, MasterCard, or American Express.

Call or write for shipping costs outside the United States.

Please allow up to two weeks for delivery within the United States.  Shipment can be made to an alternate address when purchasing this book as a gift.